The Narcissist's Journey to Healing

*A Comprehensive Self-Discovery Guide for Transforming **Ego into Empathy** to Foster and Sustain Healthy Relationships*

Joyce T.

TABLE OF CONTENTS

INTRODUCTION

First things first, thank you for being here.

It must have taken a lot of strength to be reading this right now, and I want to assure you that you've already taken the hardest step – being aware.

Everyone, whether they are a narcissist or not, finds it challenging to take a step back and assess their behaviors objectively without the inclination to make excuses for our shortcomings. We always try to "sugarcoat" the things about ourselves that we deem out of the norm, shameful, or not nice.

Now, it is no secret that narcissism can cloud you and absorb every fiber of your being. So, if you are a narcissist, coming to terms with your shortcomings is possibly the hardest thing you can do – but it doesn't mean that it can't be done.

In light of this, we're about to take a journey together, a journey to uncover parts of yourself that may feel a little uncomfortable. It might be a little bumpy at times, but that's okay because we're in this together.

Why does this matter now, you ask? It's because we're living in an age where self-focus is at an all-time high. Social media, the selfie culture, the relentless pursuit of success - they're all feeding into this. But here's the thing: it's not too late to change. We can learn to shift our focus from 'me' to 'we' from ego to empathy. And I believe, with all my heart, that this book can help you do that.

This book is your prelude to understanding narcissism. We'll break down what it means to be a narcissist, why it happens, and how it impacts relationships. But more than that, we'll explore strategies and practical steps to transform these tendencies.

As we embark on this journey together, know it won't be a walk in the park. There may be moments of discomfort, moments where you confront parts of yourself that you've been avoiding. But remember that growth often comes from discomfort. And I'll be with you every step of the way, sharing insights, exercises, and stories from my own personal journey.

So, are you ready to take this leap? Let's dive in.

Chapter 1

THE NARCISSIST WITHIN

1

Narcissism is often misunderstood.

It is seen as this flashy "character trait" where the person in question is entirely self-absorbed and doesn't give other people the time of day. This is one of the reasons why most people have a hard time accepting that they may be a narcissist. I mean, why would you? You can be kind when required to be, treat people fairly nicely, and are the least flashy person out there. But the truth is, narcissism goes beyond the surface.

It's a complex web of behaviors, attitudes, and beliefs that can cause a lot of pain, not just for the person with narcissistic tendencies but also for the people around them.

So, you're ready to truly comprehend narcissism. Great! We'll start with a fundamental question: what is narcissism, really?

1.1 Narcissism: An Overview

Narcissism, in its simplest form, refers to an inflated sense of self-importance and an intense focus on oneself. It's like looking through a magnifying glass where you, and only you, become the center of the universe.

Definition and Origin

Let's dig a bit deeper. The term 'Narcissism' originates from the ancient Greek myth of Narcissus, a handsome young man who fell so in love with his reflection in a pool of water that he couldn't look away, ultimately leading to his demise. Quite a dramatic tale, isn't it? But it perfectly illustrates the concept of narcissism: an excessive fascination with oneself.

In psychological terms, narcissism is seen as a personality trait where a person has a grandiose sense of self-importance, lacks empathy for others, and has an insatiable need for admiration.

Now, you might be thinking, "This doesn't sound like me. I'm not that self-absorbed." But here's the catch: narcissism isn't just about being self-obsessed. It's a spectrum, ranging from healthy self-esteem at one end to a full-blown narcissistic personality disorder at the other. And guess what? We all fall somewhere on this spectrum.

According to the National Institute of Health, approximately 6.2% of adults in the U.S. have Narcissistic Personality Disorder (NPD), with rates as high as 7.7% in men and 4.8% in women. That's a significant chunk of the population dealing with some degree of narcissism.

Common Misconceptions

Narcissism is not just about vanity or arrogance. It's not about being a "bad" person. Narcissism is a complex trait that can manifest in a variety of ways, often rooted in early life experiences and coping mechanisms.

One of the biggest misconceptions is that narcissists are full of self-love. In reality, this inflated self-image often masks deep-seated insecurities and self-doubt. It's more like a coping mechanism to protect themselves from a perceived threat.

Another misconception is that narcissists don't care about others. While it's true that they may struggle with empathy, this doesn't mean they are incapable of caring. Their ability to connect with others might be buried under layers of self-protection, but with effort and understanding, it can be unearthed.

Now that we have a basic understanding of what narcissism is, we can start to explore it in more depth.

The next step here will be trying to understand where narcissism stems from.

1.2. The Root Cause

Research is pretty clear, there's no gene for NPD. So, we've established that you were certainly not born a narcissist. Now the question is, at what point did these traits slowly make their way into your personality?

Environmentally Charged

Whether we like it or not, our environment, including the people we interact with on a personal level, molds our perception of self. When we are young and fully dependent on our parents, we also depend on them to show us how to act, treat ourselves, and treat others. So, most likely, this is where narcissism is birthed in most cases. Usually, when a parent overly praises their child or overly criticizes them, this can lead to narcissism (no extreme is better than the other).

How?

Excess Praise	Excess Judgment
Excess praise, especially when it's not warranted, may lead a child to believe that they are more special than others and are entitled to privileges.	When a parent lacks warmth toward their child, isn't affectionate, and criticizes them often, it can lead to them trying to put themselves on a pedestal to obtain the approval they lacked with their parents.

Now, we will couple this book with a little self-reflection just to try and absorb the information as we keep reading; trust me, I understand that this can be a lot to take in.

In light of the above, which side of the table sounds more like your parents?

____

____

____

____

____

____

____

As we work through the rest of the book, I need you to keep this one fact in mind: you are not a bad person. You are simply a reflection of your upbringing, but while you didn't have any control then, you can take control now and turn things around.

Narcissism Post-Toxic Relationships

Sometimes, someone who has never exhibited narcissistic traits may begin to do so after being in a relationship with a narcissist. This happens as a coping mechanism trying to sort of "outplay" the narcissist, and in the process, you may temporarily acquire these traits.

It may also be because they may have eroded your self-identity or pushed past your boundaries, and with a blurred identity, you may adopt the traits of the person closest to you at the moment – them.

The good thing about this kind of acquired narcissism is that it is easier to eliminate. Your true sense of self is still in there, and with a little help, which you will find in this book, you can bring back the real you.

1.3 The Spectrum of Narcissism: Overt and Covert

There's a fascinating complexity to narcissism, much like a rainbow that emerges after a storm. It's not just one color, one shade, or one pattern. It's a spectrum. On this spectrum, two types stand out: overt and covert narcissism.

Characteristics of Overt Narcissism

Think of overt narcissism as the loud, flashy car on a silent street. It's hard to miss. As an overt narcissist, you tend to be outwardly self-centered, with what people may call a heightened sense of self-importance. You also have no problem with being in the spotlight and expecting others to admire and praise you.

Let's break it down a bit more. Overt narcissists generally:

- Believe they are superior and unique, expecting others to recognize their greatness.

- Require constant admiration and affirmation from others.

- Display a sense of entitlement, expecting special treatment.

- Use others to achieve their own goals, showing little regard for others' feelings or needs.

- Display arrogance and haughty behaviors, often belittling others to elevate themselves.

Think of a situation where you've interacted with someone who dominated the conversation, constantly steering it back to their achievements, experiences, and life. Maybe they dismissed your opinion, or worse, didn't even ask for it. Ring any bells? That's overt narcissism in action.

Traits of Covert Narcissism

On the other hand, covert narcissism is a little trickier to identify. It's like a sleek, black sports car whizzing past at night. You might not see it, but you'll feel the breeze as it speeds by. Covert narcissists, also known as vulnerable or closet narcissists, share many traits with their overt counterparts but in a less obvious manner.

Here's what covert narcissism often looks like:

- They harbor fantasies about their own intelligence, beauty, success, or power, but these are more hidden and less obvious.

- They are hypersensitive to how others perceive them and fear being considered inferior.

- They often feel misunderstood or unappreciated, believing others fail to recognize their greatness.

- They may play the victim or the martyr, craving sympathy or admiration.

- They display passive-aggressive behaviors, often expressing their anger or resentment in indirect ways.

Imagine you're at a gathering, and there's someone quietly sitting in a corner. They don't engage much, but when they do, their comments are subtly self-praising or belittling towards others. They may complain that no one appreciates their hard work or understands their complex thoughts. This is your covert narcissist.

Take a breather and do a bit of self-reflection below. Between a covert and overt narcissist, which sounds more like you and why?

____

____

____

____

____

____

Differences and Similarities

So, how do these two types compare? Well, overt narcissists are like an open book with large, bold letters. They wear their narcissism on their sleeve, making it evident to everyone around them. They are the 'classic' narcissists that most people think of when they hear the term.

Covert narcissists, in contrast, are like a mystery novel with small, intricate print. They keep their narcissism hidden, revealing it only in certain situations or to certain people. They may even appear shy or reserved to the outside world, but underneath, they harbor the same grandiose fantasies and feelings of entitlement as overt narcissists.

Despite these differences, both types share a critical trait: a lack of empathy. Whether overt or covert, you may struggle to step into someone else's shoes, to genuinely understand and share their feelings. This lack of empathy is at the core of many of the challenges you face, from strained relationships to personal dissatisfaction.

As we unravel the complexities of narcissism, it's important to remember that everyone is unique. Not everyone will fit neatly into the 'overt' or 'covert' box. Many people may display a mix of traits, or their behaviors may change depending on the situation or over time.

The key is to understand these patterns, to recognize them in ourselves and others, and to use this understanding for positive change.

1.4 Narcissism and Self-Awareness: The First Step

Self-awareness is the mirror that reflects our true selves. It's the ability to look inward, to see ourselves as we indeed are, not as we wish to be or fear we might be. It's the key to unlocking our potential and path to personal growth. And when it comes to narcissism, self-awareness is the starting point of transformation.

Importance of Self-Awareness

For narcissists, self-awareness isn't just important; it's paramount. Why? Because narcissism, by its very nature, is a distortion of self-perception. It's like looking at oneself through a funhouse mirror that magnifies some traits (like self-importance) and minimizes others (like empathy).

Self-awareness helps correct this distortion. It allows us to see ourselves clearly and honestly. It peels back the layers of self-deception and denial, revealing the true nature of our thoughts, feelings, and behaviors.

Moreover, self-awareness can help you understand the impact of your actions on others. Here, you can see how an intense need for admiration, a sense of entitlement, or a lack of empathy affects your relationships. This understanding can be a powerful motivator for change.

Self-Assessment Techniques

So, how does one cultivate self-awareness? Here are a few techniques that can help:

- **Mindfulness:** Mindfulness is the practice of being present, of focusing on the here and now. It involves paying attention to your thoughts, feelings, and behaviors without judgment.

You can tailor mindfulness to your current circumstances and goals by being mindful of your inner talk and how you treat others. Whenever you are interacting with someone, ask yourself questions such as:

Did I say something offensive?

Did I give them ample time to respond, or did I just cut them off?

Am I really listening to what they are saying and understanding it?

Was what I said truthful, *or did I say it to try to modify reality?*

Also, stay on top of your inner self-talk. We often have thoughts about ourselves, and if you have narcissistic tendencies, you are aware of how yours may look like. In this case, don't be afraid to ask for a logical explanation when your mind tells you, say, something like, *"You are the best partner he/she will ever have."*

- **Journaling:** Writing can be a powerful tool for building your self-awareness. It allows you to express your thoughts and feelings freely, without fear of judgment or criticism. Try to set aside a few minutes each day to write about your experiences, reactions, fears, dreams, etc.

But you have to journal with a purpose. The point is to try to find patterns in your behavior. There's no point in filling your journal with how awesome you are, now is there?

As you journal, sieve through the mental chatter that often comes with narcissism and write from the perspective of a nonjudgmental observer.

Over time, you might be able to see patterns that will paint a pretty clear picture of your behavior.

- **Feedback from Others:** Sometimes, we're too close to our own behavior to see it clearly. That's where feedback from others can be invaluable. Reach out to trusted friends, family members, or a therapist and ask for their honest feedback. Remember, the goal isn't to defend yourself or justify your actions but to understand and learn.

Sure, they may say things that feel like a kick to the gut, but instead of being defensive, thank them and analyze what they are saying from their perspective.

- **Therapy:** If you feel like you are having a hard time grasping your sense of self, working with a professional therapist can provide a safe, supportive environment to explore your narcissistic traits. A skilled therapist can guide you in examining your behaviors, understanding their roots, and developing strategies for change.

Recognizing Narcissistic Traits

Recognizing narcissistic traits in oneself can be a challenging task. It requires a willingness to look beyond the surface to acknowledge behaviors and attitudes that might be uncomfortable or even painful to admit.

A good starting point is to revisit the characteristics of narcissism we discussed earlier.

Do you often feel superior to others?

Do you crave constant admiration and affirmation?

Do you frequently belittle or dismiss others to boost your own self-esteem?

If so, these could be signs of narcissistic tendencies.

It's also important to pay attention to your reactions in different situations.

Do you become defensive when criticized?

Do you feel envious when others succeed?

Do you struggle to empathize with others' feelings?

These reactions can provide valuable clues about your narcissistic traits.

Remember, recognizing these traits isn't about labeling yourself as a "bad" person or beating yourself up. It's about understanding yourself better, acknowledging your strengths and weaknesses, and taking steps towards positive change.

Activity

Do you recognize any of the above narcissistic traits? Write them down and any other traits you think you may exhibit:

____

____

____

____

____

____

____

____

At this point, you might feel a mix of emotions: surprise, confusion, and even a bit of discomfort. That's perfectly normal. Remember, self-awareness is a process, not a destination. It's about continuous learning and growth. So, take a deep breath, give yourself a pat on the back for taking this first step, and prepare for the next part of the process.

1.5 The Narcissism and Empathy Disconnect

Now that we've looked at narcissism and self-awareness, it's time to address another critical aspect: empathy. This is the ability to understand and share the feelings of others, to put yourself in someone else's shoes.

It's the glue that holds relationships together, the bridge that connects us to others. But for narcissists, this bridge often seems to be missing. So, let's figure out why and how we can build it.

Understanding Empathy

Think of empathy as a radio. It allows us to tune into others' frequencies, hear their thoughts, feel their emotions, and understand their experiences. Just as a radio has different channels, empathy has different forms:

- Cognitive Empathy: This is about understanding someone else's thoughts and perspectives. It's like being an excellent detective, picking up clues and piecing together the puzzle of someone else's mind.

- Emotional Empathy: This form of empathy is about sharing someone else's feelings. When they're happy, you feel happy. When they're sad, you feel sad. It's like being an emotional mirror, reflecting back what the other person is feeling.

- Compassionate Empathy: This is the most active form of empathy. It involves understanding and sharing someone else's feelings and being moved to help if needed. It's like being a good friend, ready to lend a hand or offer a shoulder to lean on.

Empathy is a vital skill and a cornerstone of healthy, fulfilling relationships. But for narcissists, this skill often seems out of reach.

Why Narcissists Struggle with Empathy

Imagine trying to tune into a radio station, but all you get is static. That's what empathy often feels like for narcissists. They struggle to pick up other people's signals to tune into their frequencies. This isn't because they're incapable of empathy. Rather, it's because their own signals - their own needs and desires - are so loud that they drown out everything else.

Narcissists often struggle with empathy for a few reasons:

- Self-focus: Narcissists are usually so focused on their own needs and wants that they struggle to perceive others'. It's like trying to hear a whisper in a rock concert.

- Insecurity: Deep down, many narcissists feel insecure and unworthy. Empathizing with others requires vulnerability, which can trigger these hidden insecurities.

- Fear of Losing Control: Narcissists often fear that showing empathy will make them appear weak or lose control. They see relationships as hierarchical and believe that to stay on top; they must maintain an image of superiority and invulnerability.

But here's the good news: Narcissists can learn to be more empathetic. It takes time, effort, and patience, but it's possible. And it starts with cultivating self-awareness and understanding the value of empathy.

Before we start cultivating empathy, let's do a little assessment to see just how empathetic you are/not.

1. Imagine a close friend is going through a tough time; for example, they got fired. How would you approach supporting them emotionally?

____

____

2. Think about a recent disagreement or conflict you had with someone. How did you try to understand their perspective and emotions during that situation? Did you make an effort to see things from their point of view, and if so, how?

3. How do you typically react when you see someone expressing strong emotions, such as joy, sadness, or frustration?

____

____

____

____

____

____

4. When making decisions that could impact others, do you take their feelings and concerns into account?

____

____

____

____

____

Strategies to Cultivate Empathy

Cultivating empathy is like learning a new language. It might feel strange and awkward at first, but with practice, it becomes more natural.

Here are a few strategies that can help:

- Active Listening: This involves not just hearing but listening to what the other person is saying. It's about paying attention to their words, tone of voice, and body language. It's about not only showing that you're interested and engaged but also taking in what is being said.

- Perspective-Taking: This involves putting yourself in someone else's shoes and trying to see things from their point of view. It's not about agreeing with them or dismissing your own perspective but about understanding their thoughts and feelings.

- Emotional Regulation: This involves managing your own emotions so that they don't interfere with your ability to empathize. It's about learning to stay calm and centered, even when dealing with difficult or uncomfortable feelings.

- Practicing Mindfulness: This involves being present in the moment, focusing on your thoughts, feelings, and sensations without judgment. It can help you tune into your own emotions and those of others.

Just like learning to be self-aware, building empathy is a journey, not a destination. It's a skill that can be developed and strengthened over time, and ultimately, it will help you build deeper connections and understanding.

So, as we wrap up this exploration of narcissism, remember this: Change is possible. Growth is possible. And you have the power to make it happen. Whether you're dealing with narcissistic tendencies or trying to understand a loved one who is, remember that you're not alone.

Take it one step at a time and you've got this.

Chapter 2

UNMASKING THE NARCISSIST: IMPACT AND INFLUENCE

2

This chapter will provide an intimate look into your perspective of the world, self, others, and relationships through the lens of narcissism. We'll also explore how these perceptions influence your behavior and life.

2.1 The Narcissist's World: A Close-Up

Let's start by zooming in on your perception of self. In the world of a narcissist, the self stands tall like a grand castle—towering and majestic. You perceive yourself as unique, superior, and deserving of special treatment. This elevated self-perception can manifest in various ways. For instance, you might believe in your exceptional intelligence, attractiveness, or talents even when evidence suggests otherwise. It's common to claim credit for successes that may not entirely be yours or to exaggerate achievements to appear more impressive occasionally.

However, it's important to acknowledge that even within the grandeur, there are often deep-seated insecurities and moments of self-doubt. It's a complex interplay between the exterior projection and the internal vulnerabilities that make up the intricate landscape of a narcissist's self-perception.

Narcissist's Perception of Others

In your world, other people may feel like chess pieces on a board. They are there to be moved, manipulated, and used to help you achieve your goals. You often view others in terms of what they can offer - admiration, validation, resources - rather than who they are as individuals.

This objectifying perception can lead to a lack of genuine interest in others' thoughts, feelings, or experiences. Imagine having a conversation with someone who constantly steers the topic back to themselves, dismisses your opinions, or shows little regard for your feelings. That's what interacting with a narcissist can feel like.

However, this doesn't mean that you are incapable of caring for others. You can and do form attachments, but unfortunately, these are often conditional and based on how well the other person caters to your needs and desires.

Narcissist's Perception of Relationships

In the realm of relationships, you may sometimes perceive them as a means to fulfill your needs and enhance your self-esteem, akin to a farmer caring for a crop, providing just enough attention for a bountiful harvest.

In a relationship, you might shower your partner with affection and attention initially, a phase often referred to as 'love bombing.' However, this affection often wanes over time, especially if your partner fails to meet your high expectations or demands for admiration.

You may also struggle with boundaries in relationships. There could be instances where personal space is invaded, feelings are dismissed, or manipulation is employed to achieve your objectives, resembling a bulldozer plowing through obstacles.

However, it's important to remember that you, like everyone else, are capable of change. With self-awareness, effort, and professional help, you can learn to build healthier, more balanced relationships.

In this section, we've seen that your perceptions of self, others, and relationships are highly influenced by your self-image, sense of entitlement, and lack of empathy. These perceptions tend to impact behavior, sometimes resulting in patterns of manipulation, dominance, and unintentional disregard for others' needs and feelings.

2.2 The Ripple Effect: Narcissism and Relationships

To truly recognize the impact of narcissism in your life, I will need you to view this part as a silent observer. It's always easier to see other people's faults than it is to see our own. So, as you read through the next few sections, view this narcissistic aspect of yourself as an outsider.

Impact on Romantic Relationships

Narcissism in romantic relationships is like a firework display. It begins with a bang - a dazzling display of affection, charm, and grand gestures. This phase, often termed 'love bombing' as we've seen, is designed to captivate and charm your partner. But as with a firework display, the spectacle doesn't last.

Over time, the relationship can become a one-way street, with the narcissistic partner demanding constant attention and admiration. Their needs, desires, and expectations take center stage, often at the expense of their partner's feelings and needs.

Criticism, even if constructive, can trigger defensiveness or aggression in the narcissist. They might resort to blame-shifting, gaslighting, or emotional manipulation to avoid confronting their own shortcomings.

Intimacy, both emotional and physical, can be a challenge. While narcissists often crave the validation that comes with intimacy, they also fear the vulnerability it requires. This push-pull dynamic can create a turbulent, unstable relationship environment.

Effect on Friendships

In friendships, narcissists often seek individuals who admire and validate them. They're drawn to friends who bolster their self-image and cater to their needs.

These friendships can seem perfectly normal on the surface, but cracks often appear over time.

Narcissists may struggle to reciprocate the attention and support they receive. They might dismiss their friends' problems or turn the conversation back to themselves. Over time, this one-sided dynamic can strain the friendship, leading to conflict or distance.

Furthermore, narcissists often struggle with jealousy, viewing their friends' successes as a threat to their self-esteem. They might belittle their friends' achievements or exaggerate their own to maintain their sense of superiority.

Influence on Family Dynamics

Our families are our first social circle, the place where we learn to interact, share, and connect. But when a family member is a narcissist, these lessons can become skewed.

Narcissism can disrupt family dynamics in various ways. The narcissistic family member often demands constant attention and admiration from their relatives. They might impose their expectations and standards on others, often leading to conflict.

Narcissists may also play family members against each other, a tactic known as 'triangulation'. By creating rivalries or alliances, they can manipulate family dynamics to serve their own needs.

Moreover, narcissists often struggle with empathy, making it difficult for them to understand or respect their family members' feelings. This lack of empathy can lead to communication breakdowns, misunderstandings, and emotional distance.

It's clear that narcissism can significantly impact relationships, creating ripples of disruption and discontent. But it's important to remember that these patterns aren't set in stone. With awareness, effort, and professional help, if needed, it's possible to navigate these challenges and build healthier, more balanced relationships.

2.3 Narcissism at Work: Professional Implications

In the professional realm, narcissism can be a double-edged sword, cutting both ways in how it shapes and influences work dynamics. Let's take a closer look.

Narcissism and Leadership

A corner office, a seat at the head of the conference table, a team hanging on every word - for some narcissists, these are the trappings of a dream job. Leadership roles can be a magnet for narcissists, offering ample opportunities to bask in the spotlight and exert influence over others.

A narcissistic leader often makes a strong first impression. Their confidence and charisma can be magnetic, drawing others towards them. They may present grand visions and bold strategies, inspiring their team to strive for lofty goals.

However, beneath this shiny veneer, the reality can be less than ideal. Narcissistic leaders often prioritize their own needs and ambitions over those of their team. They may take credit for others' work, dismiss valuable input, and respond poorly to criticism.

This self-centric approach can create a hierarchical, competitive work environment. Instead of fostering collaboration and mutual growth, narcissistic leaders may breed a culture of fear and constant one-upmanship.

Narcissism and Teamwork

Narcissists often struggle with teamwork. Their need for dominance and recognition can lead them to overshadow or undermine their colleagues. They may hoard information, take sole credit for team achievements, or blame others for failures.

Their lack of empathy can also make it challenging to collaborate effectively. They may dismiss their colleagues' ideas, belittle their efforts, or ignore their concerns. This can lead to conflict, low morale, and decreased productivity.

Narcissism and Work Performance

Imagine a high-wire artist performing without a safety net. The thrill of the risk, the roar of the crowd, the glory of the spotlight - it's a heady mix that many narcissists find irresistible. And just like the high-wire artist, narcissists often perform exceptionally well under pressure.

However, this high-risk, high-reward approach can also be their downfall. When things go well, narcissists can be stellar performers, their confidence and ambition propelling them to great heights. But when things go wrong, their performance can plummet.

Narcissists often struggle with criticism and failure, seeing them as threats to their self-image. Instead of learning from these experiences, they may deny their mistakes, blame others, or deflect criticism. This can hinder their ability to grow and adapt, ultimately affecting their work performance.

Also, narcissists' focus on individual success can lead them to neglect their responsibilities toward their team or organization. They may prioritize personal gain over collective goals, damaging team cohesion and organizational culture.

In the realm of work, narcissism is like a potent spice. In small doses, it can add flavor and zest. But too much can overpower the dish, throwing everything off balance.

The question is, in a work setting, how do you interact with others, and what's your work conduct?

____

____

____

____

____

____

____

2.4 Narcissism and Self-Destruction: The Hidden Cost

Emotional Toll of Narcissism

Imagine yourself on a roller coaster, experiencing dizzying heights, stomach-churning drops, and gut-wrenching turns. This mirrors a day in your emotional life as a narcissist. It's important to recognize that narcissism can take a significant emotional toll, leading to a continuous state of emotional turmoil.

You may often experience intense emotions but struggle to manage them effectively. They can swing from feelings of grandiosity and invincibility to despair and worthlessness. The constant need for validation and fear of criticism can lead to anxiety, depression, and emotional instability.

Moreover, lacking genuine connections and empathy can lead to a profound sense of loneliness and isolation. Despite everything, you may often feel disconnected and misunderstood, creating a chasm of emptiness within.

Physical Health Implications

Research suggests that narcissists may be more prone to health issues due to their lifestyle and coping mechanisms. The constant stress and emotional turmoil can affect your sleep, diet, and overall well-being. You may resort to risky behaviors or substance abuse as a way to cope with emotional pain or to maintain your self-image.

Moreover, narcissists often struggle with health-seeking behaviors. Your fear of appearing weak or vulnerable might prevent you from seeking medical help or following through with treatment plans. This can exacerbate existing health issues and lead to poor health outcomes.

Impact on Personal Growth and Development

Consider a tree growing in a pot, its roots confined, unable to spread, and draw nourishment from the soil. This is a bit like the personal growth of a narcissist, hindered by some level of a self-centered worldview and a struggle with empathy.

You may often struggle with self-improvement and personal development. An inflated self-perception leaves little room for acknowledging flaws or learning from mistakes. You tend to see feedback or criticism as threats, missing opportunities for growth and learning.

Moreover, your focus on external validation and success often overshadows your personal growth. You may neglect your emotional health, interpersonal skills, and character development, prioritizing your image over your integrity.

Think about this for a second: is there a point in your life where you've ever been so focused on success or your self-image in general that your health, whether physical, emotional, or mental, suffered?

Besides this, a lack of genuine empathy can hinder your social and emotional intelligence, limiting your ability to build healthy, fulfilling relationships. This can stunt your personal growth and lead to a sense of stagnation and dissatisfaction.

As we turn the page to the next chapter, we'll explore more about some tactics that you may knowingly or unknowingly use that are considered narcissistic. The reason for exploring this? So that you can have the capacity to know when your actions are manipulative and understand when to stop.

Chapter 3

THE NARCISSIST'S PLAYBOOK: TACTICS AND STRATEGIES

3

For this part of our journey, we are going to dive deeper into how narcissism actually manifests. Now, you may read somethings and instantly be like, "Yeah, I definitely do that." And you may read some and not recognize any of it in you. Either way, I suggest that you approach this just as you have with the rest of the book.

View the tactics from an outsider's perspective and try to recall any instance that you may have used a tactic or when you've ever been accused of the same.

Ideally, the "playground" of narcissism often looks like this:

Imagine yourself stepping into a grand theater, where the curtain rises to reveal a captivating drama centered around narcissism. The storyline unfolds with a series of manipulative tactics and strategies that subtly distort reality, often leaving others in a state of confusion and self-doubt.

Now, get ready as we shine a light on these tactics, starting with one particularly sneaky maneuver: gaslighting.

3.1 Gaslighting: Twisting Reality

"I have no idea what you're talking about. That never happened. You must be imagining things."

"You're being overly sensitive. I was just joking, and now you're making a big deal out of nothing. It's not my fault if you can't take a joke."

"I can't have a reasonable conversation with you when you're so *emotional.* Maybe you should take a step back and calm down."

This is what gaslighting sounds like: denial, shifting blame, and minimizing feelings.

If you recognize any of the above statements, you have a general idea of what I'm talking about here. Let's look at such statements in depth.

Denial of Past Actions

Have you ever found yourself in a conversation where the other person flatly denies an event or action that you distinctly remember? It's like being in a surreal game where the rules constantly change, leaving you disoriented and doubting your memory. This is a classic gaslighting move. Here, you may deny past actions or experiences, insisting they never happened or were significantly different from how the other person remembers them.

Let's say, for instance, you are confronted about a disparaging comment you made about someone in a meeting. Instead of acknowledging it, you flatly deny such a comment was made, making the other person question their memory and perception.

While this gives you an easy escape from facing the consequences of your actions, it can mentally and emotionally harm the other person.

Discrediting Others' Perceptions

Now, picture yourself sharing your thoughts and feelings with someone, only to have them dismissed or belittled. Frustrating, isn't it? Narcissists often use this gaslighting technique to invalidate others' perceptions, making them feel irrational or overly sensitive.

For instance, you might scoff at a friend's concern about your manipulative behavior, labeling it as an overreaction. Here, you can say things like, "You're too sensitive" or "You're reading too much into it," effectively invalidating their feelings and experiences.

Manipulating Emotions

You may use gaslighting to manipulate other people's emotions, creating an atmosphere of uncertainty and self-doubt – which can ultimately make the other person distrust their own emotions.

For example, you might instigate an argument and then blame your partner for the conflict. You might accuse them of being 'too emotional' or 'not understanding you, making them feel guilty and confused. And eventually, they can start believing they are "too emotional" or "not understanding."

As we lift the curtain on these manipulative tactics, it's important to remember that knowledge is power. Understanding these strategies equips us to identify and counteract them, fostering healthier interactions and relationships. By shining a spotlight on the stage of narcissistic manipulation, we can see the actors, understand the plot, and change the ending of the story.

3.2 Projection: The Blame Game

In your world, accepting blame may feel like conceding defeat. Taking responsibility may feel like a challenge to your self-image, a potential imperfection. You may have developed a knack for redirecting blame to sidestep this discomfort, almost like a skilled player passing the ball at just the right moment. This could manifest in various ways, from openly attributing your mistakes to others to subtly pointing out the shortcomings of those around you to divert attention from your own.

Accusing Others of Own Faults

Ever had an interaction where someone accused you of the very thing they were guilty of? This can be one of the most triggering and frustrating situations out there.

Here, you can find yourself accusing others of the attitudes, behaviors, or traits they refuse to acknowledge in yourself. It's like you're in a boxing ring, punching your own shadow. For instance, you might accuse someone of being selfish when you are the ones neglecting their needs, or you might label someone as arrogant when you are the one displaying superiority.

It's a classic case of "the pot calling the kettle black."

Avoiding Self-Reflection

Let's consider a river, its waters running deep and fast. The surface reflects the world around it, but what lies beneath remains unseen. This represents the narcissist's self-reflection. You avoid looking beneath the surface, fearing what you might find.

Self-reflection requires honesty, vulnerability, and a willingness to confront one's flaws - things that challenge your self-image. Projection serves as a defense mechanism, a mirror that reflects your faults onto others, sparing you the discomfort of self-examination.

For instance, you might repeatedly accuse your partner of being unfaithful while you are engaging in infidelity. By focusing on your partner's supposed faults, you avoid facing your own guilt.

3.3 Triangulation: Divide and Conquer

As humans, we are social creatures, but for a narcissist, strong social connections between them and the people close to them are seen as a threat. A threat to their control and a threat to their position in other people's lives.

In light of that, you may use the following tactics to sever connections:

Creating Rivalries

Picture a game of chess. Each piece has its role, its moves, and its power. But what if the player begins to pit the pieces against each other, creating tension and rivalry on the board? This is precisely how a narcissist operates when creating rivalries.

In a social setting, you might share selective information or spread rumors to incite conflict between others, ensuring you remain the sought-after ally or the voice of reason. For instance, you might praise one team member's idea to another but then critique it to someone else, causing confusion and competition. In such a scenario, you thrive, sitting back and enjoying the show, always in control of the narrative.

Manipulating Relationships

Here, you might use the classic 'divide and rule' strategy, which involves undermining relationships between others to reinforce your own position.

For instance, in a family setting, a narcissistic parent might favor one child over another, manipulating their relationships to maintain control.

By positioning themselves as the coveted favorite, they ensure a constant supply of attention and validation.

Maintaining Control

Think about a conductor leading an orchestra, each wave of the baton controlling the tempo, the volume, the harmony. This is how a narcissist maintains control using triangulation. Basically, you set the tempo of interactions, control the volume of conflict, and disrupt the harmony when it suits you.

A narcissistic boss, for instance, might involve a third party in a discussion or decision, complicating the dynamics and ensuring they remain in control. They may use this tactic to deflect criticism, evade responsibility, or simply assert their dominance.

Triangulation is a sophisticated tactic, one designed to maintain power and control. It's a strategy that thrives on confusion, tension, and rivalry, leaving others second-guessing their perceptions, doubting their relationships, and constantly seeking your approval.

3.4 Love Bombing and Devaluation: The Narcissist's Cycle

Two of the most commonly used tactics by narcissists are love bombing and devaluation, which follow a pattern – this can be referred to as a narcissist's cycle.

Let's see how this cycle unfolds in this section:

Initial Overwhelming Affection

Love bombing feels like this:

During this stage, you're showered with attention, every wish granted before you can even voice it, every insecurity soothed with honeyed words. It feels like a dream, a fairy tale spun just for you.

For you, the ability to do this seems to come effortlessly. You have a way of captivating others with your charm, charisma, and intense affection. You skillfully reflect back their deepest desires, creating a profound sense of being seen, understood, and loved.

In your world, they become everything—the sun, the moon, the stars. It's an intoxicating experience, a whirlwind romance like no other.

Sudden Criticism and Disapproval

After the serenity of the initial stage, the second stage sets in, which feels like this:

But, just as you're basking in this glow, the scenery shifts. The roses wither, the praises turn into criticisms, the grand gestures into grand disappointments. Where once you could do no wrong, now you can do no right. Every flaw, every mistake, every shortcoming is magnified, dissected, and thrown back at you. It's jarring, confusing, like a sudden plunge into icy waters.

This is the second act - devaluation. Here, you may begin to indirectly or unknowingly chip away at the other person's self-esteem, confidence, and sense of self. This can be through belittling their achievements, dismissing their feelings, and undermining their worth.

Emotional Withdrawal

And then, the climax is emotional withdrawal. Here, you will pull away, your affection drying up like a desert stream. You become distant and indifferent; your once warm gaze is now cold and dismissive, and the other person is left in the shadows, scrambling for the scraps of your attention, love, and approval.

The withdrawal can be as subtle as neglecting their needs or as overt as ignoring their existence. It's a power play, a game of control where you hold all the cards, leaving them in a state of uncertainty, walking on eggshells, always on edge.

Repeating the Cycle

Finally, the cycle repeats itself. Just when they're ready to walk away, you pull them back in, reigniting the love bombing stage. The cycle of overwhelming affection, sudden devaluation, and emotional withdrawal starts anew, keeping the other person in a perpetual state of confusion and emotional tumult.

And so, the cycle ends, only to begin again.

But this time, it doesn't have to. In the next chapter we will see how you can move from ego to empathy.

But before that, answer this question: Do you recognize any part of this cycle?

Chapter 4

FROM EGO TO EMPATHY: THE NARCISSIST'S TRANSFORMATION

4

Imagine being trapped inside a glass bubble. You can see the world outside, but you can't touch it, feel it, or connect with it. This is often how you experience your emotions - visible but untouchable.

But what if we could break that bubble? What if we could bridge the gap between you and your emotions, turning fear into courage, insecurity into confidence, and defensiveness into openness? That's what this chapter is all about - unlocking the door to emotional vulnerability and empathy.

Now picture yourself on a tightrope, high above the ground. On one side, there's the fear of rejection, a gust of wind that could knock you off balance. On the other side, there's the need for validation, a safety net that promises to catch you if you fall. And right in the middle, balancing precariously, is you.

4.1 Complicated Emotions: Narcissism and Vulnerability

You are not a bad person. Even if you've gone through this book so far and realized that you might indeed be a narcissist, don't brand yourself as a bad person.

Below are some of the reasons why vulnerability feels as if you are letting your guard down, leaving you open for attack.

Fear of Rejection

Rejection is a bitter pill to swallow for most of us, but for you, it might feel like poison. It goes against your self-image, shattering the illusion of perfection you strive to maintain. Rejection is not just a setback - it's a threat to your very identity. It brings to the surface your deepest fear: that you just might not be as exceptional as you believe yourself to be.

This fear often manifests in your relationships and interactions. You might avoid situations where you risk rejection, such as asking for a promotion or expressing your feelings. Alternatively, you might react with anger or defensiveness when faced with rejection, blaming others to protect your self-esteem.

Need for Validation

Imagine standing in a desert, feeling parched and desperately longing for a drop of water. That's similar to your yearning for validation—it's like a lifeline, your elixir. Validation serves as confirmation for your grandiose self-perception and offers reassurance of your inherent worth. It satisfies your thirst for recognition and admiration.

Yet, this continual need for validation may inadvertently foster emotional dependence on others. Seeking compliments, affirmation, or attention becomes a common practice, and your sense of self-worth becomes intertwined with external feedback. This reliance can lead to a rollercoaster of emotions, with your self-esteem fluctuating with each wave of validation or criticism.

Insecurity and Defensiveness

Beneath the facade of confidence and superiority lies a complex world of emotions for many narcissists. Picture it as a fortress with towering walls shielding a fragile core. These insecurities may have roots in various factors, such as a critical parent, a traumatic event, or a history of rejection or criticism (as we covered in the initial chapter).

In an effort to safeguard yourself from these insecurities, you may adopt a defensive stance. This defensive strategy involves building an armor of arrogance, dismissiveness, and indifference to protect that vulnerable core and avoid confronting your shortcomings.

It's important to recognize the emotions that underlie narcissism. By acknowledging and addressing these fears, needs, and insecurities, you can start the process of dismantling your defensive armor. This journey involves replacing the fear of rejection with acceptance, the need for validation with self-assurance, and defensiveness with openness.

It's undoubtedly a challenging process that brings rewards—a step toward emotional freedom and genuine self-esteem.

So how can you do this? The first step is recognition. Below is a table to help you understand how you might be setting up an armor and how to let go of it. The first one is done to give you a picture of how to fill it out. Assess your own situation to help you complete it.

Defense Mechanism	Letting It Go
Maintaining emotional distance to protect against potential rejection or criticism.	Gradually open up to trusted individuals, allowing for deeper emotional connections.

4.2 The Role of Empathy in Narcissism

Picture yourself as a lighthouse, standing tall amidst turbulent seas, emitting a guiding light for passing ships. This light is empathy, a beacon that enables us to navigate the complex waters of human emotions and relationships.

For narcissists, this light often seems dim or non-existent. But the good news is, it's not a lost cause. The bulb can be replaced, the light can be rekindled, and the lighthouse can fulfill its purpose.

Understanding Others' Feelings

Imagine walking in a lively city surrounded by a sea of faces. Each face tells a story and holds a world of emotions. But often, we're too engrossed in our own world to notice. For narcissists, this is particularly challenging. Their focus is often inward, on their own feelings and needs.

But the first step towards empathy is to shift this focus outward, to tune into others' emotional frequencies. It's about observing, listening, and sensing what others are feeling. It's about moving beyond the words and understanding the emotions that underlie them.

For instance, when a friend talks about a stressful day at work, it's not just about the events they describe. It's about their feelings of frustration, their worries about performance, or their disappointment with a colleague. Understanding these emotions is the first step towards empathetic connection.

Responding Appropriately to Emotions

Now, imagine you're listening to a symphony. The music ebbs and flows, carrying a world of emotions - joy, sorrow, excitement, tranquility. As a listener, you respond to these emotions, letting them resonate within you. This is what responding to emotions is all about.

For narcissists, this can be really tricky. Your usual responses might be dismissive (e.g., "You're overreacting"), self-focused (e.g., "I never have such problems"), or even blaming (e.g., "You should have handled it better"). These responses can create a wall, blocking emotional connection.

Instead, empathetic responses involve acknowledging the other person's feelings, validating their experience, and offering support. It's about saying, "I can see you're really stressed. It sounds like you had a tough day. I'm here for you." Such responses help build bridges of understanding and connection.

Building Meaningful Connections

Finally, think of empathy as a thread, delicate yet strong, that binds us together. It's what transforms a conversation into a connection, an interaction into a relationship. For narcissists, this thread often seems elusive, but with practice, you can learn to weave it.

Building meaningful connections involves more than just understanding and responding to emotions. It's about being there consistently and authentically. It's about showing up in times of joy and sorrow, success and failure, certainty and doubt.

It's about sharing vulnerabilities and opening up about fears and insecurities. You might feel like this is a leap into the unknown. But it's a leap worth taking because the possibility of deeper, more fulfilling connections lies on the other side.

Building empathy is like planting a seed. It requires patience, care, and the right conditions to grow. There might be storms and droughts, setbacks, and challenges. But with persistence, the seed can blossom into a beautiful flower, spreading its fragrance in the garden of relationships.

So, here's to planting that seed and nurturing it with understanding, compassion, and courage. Here's to turning the glass bubble into a window that opens to a world of emotions, connections, and possibilities. Here's to transforming the ego into empathy, one step at a time.

4.3 Strategies for Building Empathy

Below are some practical strategies for building empathy:

Active Listening

Active listening involves fully concentrating on the speaker, understanding their message, responding, and then remembering the conversation. It's more than just hearing the words; it's about understanding the emotions behind them.

I know this might feel like trying to catch a butterfly - elusive and tricky. But with practice, you can learn to quiet your inner monologue to focus on the other person's words, tone, and body language. You can learn to respond with interest and understanding, creating an environment where the other person feels seen and heard.

Perspective Taking

Perspective-taking involves stepping out of your shoes and into someone else's. It's about viewing the world from their viewpoint and understanding their thoughts, feelings, and experiences.

For you, this might seem like climbing a steep hill. Your self-focused viewpoint often blocks your view of others. But with effort, you can scale this hill, broadening your view to include others' perspectives.

You can learn to pause, reflect, and ask yourself, "How might the other person be feeling? What might they be thinking? How might my actions impact them?"

Emotional Literacy

Emotional literacy involves recognizing, understanding, and expressing emotions in a healthy and constructive way. It's about expanding your emotional vocabulary, moving beyond basic labels like 'happy,' 'sad,' or 'angry' to more nuanced ones like 'excited,' 'lonely,' 'frustrated,' or 'anxious.'

This language can be a game-changer. It can help you understand your emotions and those of others. You can learn to express your feelings in a way that's respectful of your own well-being and that of others. This way, you will understand how to navigate your emotions with more confidence and ease, transforming your relationships and experiences.

To sum this up, empathy is like building a bridge. It requires a solid foundation (active listening), a strong structure (perspective taking), and a safe, reliable pathway (emotional literacy). With these elements in place, the bridge can span the gap between self and others, creating a path for understanding, connection, and growth.

So, step onto this bridge and take the first step towards a more empathetic self.

4.4 Empathy Practice: Real-Life Scenarios

Empathy is like a muscle. The more you use it, the stronger it becomes. And just like any workout, practice makes perfect. So, let's roll up our sleeves and dive into some real-life scenarios to flex our empathy muscle.

Navigating Difficult Conversations

Start by setting the stage for open, honest communication. Express your intention clearly, reassuring the other person that you're there to understand, not to judge or blame. Remember, empathy is about tuning in to their emotions, not just their words.

As the conversation unfolds, practice active listening. Pay attention to their tone of voice, their body language, and their unspoken emotions. Respond with understanding and validation, even if you don't agree with their perspective.

Finally, share your feelings and thoughts respectfully, using 'I' statements to express your viewpoint. This can help prevent the conversation from escalating into an argument, keeping the focus on understanding and resolution.

Responding to Criticism

When faced with criticism, take a moment to process your emotions. It's natural to feel defensive or upset, but reacting impulsively can worsen the situation. Instead, take a deep breath, count to ten, and remind yourself that criticism is a part of growth.

Next, listen to the feedback with an open mind. Try to understand the other person's perspective, even if it's uncomfortable. Remember, their feedback is about a specific behavior, not your worth as a person.

Finally, respond with grace and gratitude. Acknowledge their feedback, thank them for their honesty, and express your willingness to improve. This shows emotional maturity and a commitment to personal growth.

Supporting Others in Distress

Start by acknowledging their feelings. Phrases like "I can see you're really upset" or "This must be really hard for you" can validate their experience and make them feel heard.

Offer your support, both emotionally and practically. This could be as simple as a listening ear, a comforting word, or a helping hand. But remember, it's not about solving their problems; it's about providing a safe space for them to express their feelings and navigate their own solutions.

Finally, respect their pace and process. Everyone copes with distress in their own way and in their own time. Be patient, be present, and reassure them that you're there for them, no matter what.

Recognizing and Respecting Boundaries

Recognizing boundaries starts with self-awareness. Understand your own needs, limits, and comfort zones. Communicate these clearly to the other person, and be open to hearing their boundaries as well.

Respecting boundaries involves honoring these limits, even if you don't fully understand or agree with them. It's about acknowledging the other person's autonomy and treating them with respect and dignity.

Remember, boundaries are not walls meant to shut you out; they're guidelines meant to create a safe, healthy relationship. Recognizing and respecting them is a sign of emotional maturity and mutual respect.

Now that we've had our empathy workout let's take a moment to catch our breath. Practice these strategies in your daily interactions, and over time, you'll see a transformation - in your relationships, your self-esteem, and your overall well-being.

So, as we wrap up this exploration of empathy, remember this: You have the power to transform your relationships, to turn ego into empathy, to create a world that's more understanding, more compassionate, and more connected. And that, my friend, is a world worth striving for.

Next up, let's see the complete process of transformation from start to finish and how you can embrace it.

Chapter 5

EMBRACING TRANSFORMATION: TURNING THE PAGE ON NARCISSISM

5

Welcome to a new day and a fresh page. Think of it as if you are starting on a clean slate, a new blank canvas. While making amends for your past is essential, you also need not blame yourself or dwell on what you did or didn't do before. The point is to move forward and ensure that things will be different this time.

In this chapter, we're going to explore the process of transformation and the journey of turning the page on narcissism. We'll look at the stages of this journey, the milestones, the obstacles, and the victories. We'll uncover strategies to help you navigate this path, ensuring that every step brings you closer to your goal, no matter how small.

5.1 Acknowledging the Need for Change

Think of a garden that's been neglected. The weeds have taken over, the flowers have wilted, and the soil is parched. But with care, attention, and a little bit of sweat, this garden can be restored. It can bloom again, brighter and more beautiful than ever. This is the first stage of your journey: acknowledging the need for change.

Recognizing Narcissistic Traits

Let's start with the mirror. The mirror doesn't lie, doesn't flatter, doesn't judge. It simply reflects what's in front of it. This is your first step: recognizing your narcissistic traits. Take a good, hard look at yourself, not with self-criticism or judgment, but with curiosity and honesty.

Can you see the signs of narcissism? The inflated sense of self-importance, the constant need for admiration, the lack of empathy? Can you recognize the patterns in your behavior, your relationships, and your reactions? This isn't about labeling yourself as a 'narcissist' or berating yourself for your flaws. It's about understanding yourself better, acknowledging your strengths and weaknesses, and taking the first step toward change.

Accepting Feedback from Loved Ones

Now, let's turn to the people who know you best; those who care about you the most - your loved ones. They've been with you through thick and thin, seeing you at your best and worst. They're your sounding board, reality check, and compass when you lose your way.

Reach out to these people and ask for their feedback. What do they see as your strengths? Your areas for improvement? How do they experience your behavior, your attitudes, and your interactions?

Listen to their feedback, not with defensiveness or denial, but with openness and appreciation.

Remember, they're sharing their perspective because they care about you and want to support you on this journey.

Understanding the Impact on Relationships

Finally, let's consider the impact of your narcissistic traits on your relationships. Relationships are like a dance, a delicate balance of give and take, of listening and sharing, of understanding and empathy. But when one partner dominates the dance, the balance is lost, and the dance becomes a struggle.

Reflect on your relationships. How have your narcissistic traits affected your interactions with your loved ones? Has your need for admiration overshadowed their needs? Has your lack of empathy created a barrier to emotional connection? Has your fear of criticism prevented honest, open communication?

Understanding the impact of your behavior on your relationships is a crucial step in your transformation. It's a wake-up call and a motivation to change, a beacon guiding your journey towards healthier, more balanced relationships.

As we close this section, remember this: change is a choice. You have to decide to step out of your comfort zone, challenge your old patterns, and strive for a better, healthier, and happier you. It's a decision that only you can make. But you don't have to do it alone, which is why this book is here.

5.2 Elements of Change

As you embark on your journey toward change, there are a few elements that can guide you through the process. This includes:

Self-Reflection and Journaling

Imagine standing in front of a mirror, a mirror that not only reflects your physical image but also your thoughts, emotions, and actions. This mirror is self-reflection, a powerful tool that allows you to see your true self, warts and all.

Self-reflection is like a personal audit, an inventory check of your beliefs, attitudes, and behaviors. It's about asking yourself tough questions and being brave enough to face the answers.

Why do you crave constant admiration? Why do you struggle to empathize with others? What triggers your defensive behavior? These are not easy questions, but they are the keys to understanding your narcissistic traits.

Now, how do you capture these reflections? This is where journaling comes in. Think of it as a personal diary, a safe space where you can express your thoughts and feelings without judgment or fear.

We had touched on journalling a little, but basically, aim to write down:

- Your interactions with others and how different situations make you feel

- Your triggers for manifesting certain traits and how to take hold of those triggers

- A list of your self-centered thoughts and countering thoughts of gratitude

- Exploring your identity past your achievements or external validations

- Your current relationships and how to strengthen them, etc.

Therapy and Counseling

A therapist can provide a safe, supportive environment to explore your narcissistic traits. They can help you understand the root causes of your behaviors and the underlying fears and insecurities that drive your actions.

Through therapeutic techniques like Cognitive Behavioral Therapy (CBT) or Dialectical Behavior

Therapy (DBT), you can manage your emotions, improve your interpersonal skills, and build healthier coping mechanisms. Remember, it's okay to ask for help. It's not a sign of weakness but a step towards strength and genuine healing.

Building Empathy

We've already covered how to build empathy, but you have to apply it practically. Empathy as an element of change can help you move from the perception of "I" to "we." It can help you see beyond yourself as you connect with others, whether your loved ones or even strangers on a bus.

Be sure to practice empathy in your everyday interactions. Put yourself in the other person's shoes, imagine how they might feel, and respond with kindness and understanding. Remember, empathy is not about losing your identity; it's about connecting with others on a deeper, more meaningful level.

Setting Boundaries

While respecting other people's boundaries, you must also create your own. Setting boundaries is about understanding your needs, your limits, and your values. It's about communicating these clearly to others and respecting their boundaries in return.

Boundaries can be emotional (like not tolerating disrespect), physical (like needing personal space), or even digital (like not responding to emails after work hours). Remember, setting boundaries is not about pushing others away; it's about creating a safe space where respect and understanding can flourish.

Developing Emotional Intelligence

Emotional intelligence is an essential skill that can help you deal with confusing or buried emotions. It

involves recognizing, understanding, and managing your own emotions and those of others. It's about being aware of your emotional triggers, managing your emotional reactions, and effectively responding to others' emotions.

You can develop emotional intelligence by practicing mindfulness, self-reflection, and empathy.

As you can recognize, we've covered how to do all the above, so in essence, eliminating narcissism is synonymous with building your emotional intelligence.

As part of embracing change, remember to be patient with yourself. Change doesn't happen overnight. It's a process, a journey, filled with steps - some forward, some backward, but each one important. So, let's keep going.

5.3 Potential Roadblocks in the Journey

Any form of self-improvement can and will be faced with challenges. I won't lie to you; altering your way of thinking, especially a narcissistic mindset, won't be a walk in the park. There will be moments where you will be faced with complete resistance, and there will be moments where you will even feel like throwing in the towel. But in these moments, derive strength from the resistance because it shows that what you are doing has an impact on you.

Below are some of the roadblocks you will encounter and how to deal with them:

Denial and Resistance

Denial is the mind's defense mechanism against uncomfortable truths. It's like wearing rose-tinted glasses that distort your self-perception, making everything seem rosier than it is. In your case, it will manifest as a refusal to acknowledge the reality of your narcissistic traits. It's like wearing rose-tinted glasses that distort your self-perception, making everything seem rosier than it is.

Resistance, on the other hand, is a reluctance to change, even when you recognize the need for it. It's like standing at the entrance of a tunnel, knowing that you need to pass through it to reach the other side but being held back by fear, doubt, or complacency.

Overcoming denial and resistance involves courage, honesty, and determination. It's about removing the rose-tinted glasses and facing the reality of your traits and behaviors. It's about pushing against the current, knowing that every inch you move brings you closer to your goal.

Always have your goal at the back of your mind. Write it down on a sticky note and place it somewhere you will see it every day, and whenever denial or resistance kicks in, read the note for instant motivation.

Fear of Vulnerability

Vulnerability involves opening up, letting down your guard, and showing your authentic self, warts and all. For you, this can be terrifying. Your inflated self-image often serves as a protective armor, shielding you from feelings of inadequacy or inferiority.

Facing this fear requires bravery and self-compassion. It's about acknowledging that it's okay to be imperfect, to have flaws, to make mistakes. It's about realizing that vulnerability is not a weakness but a strength - a testament to your courage and your humanity.

Difficulty in Accepting Criticism

Criticism, even when constructive, can feel like an attack on your self-image. It threatens your sense of superiority and your belief in their own perfection. As a result, you might reject the criticism outright, deflect it onto others, or respond with anger or defensiveness.

Learning to accept criticism involves developing the resilience to be strong enough to listen to it and self-reflection to see past the perceived "attack.". It's about understanding that criticism is not a threat but an opportunity to learn and grow. It's about taking the bitter pill with grace, knowing that it's good for your growth.

Setbacks and Relapses

Picture yourself climbing a mountain, reaching a plateau, and then slipping back down again. This is what setbacks and relapses often feel like - a stumble on your path to the summit.

Setbacks are obstacles that slow down your progress, like old habits that resurface or situations that trigger your narcissistic behaviors. Relapses, on the other hand, are periods when you revert to your old behaviors despite your efforts to change.

Navigating these challenges involves patience, perseverance, and self-forgiveness. It's about realizing that setbacks and relapses are part of the process, not a sign of failure. It's about picking yourself up each time you stumble, dusting yourself off, and continuing your climb, one step at a time.

5.4 Celebrating Small Wins: The Power of Incremental Change

Think of yourself as a gardener, tending a plot of land. Each day, you water the seeds, remove the weeds, and watch for signs of growth. Some days, you may see a bud blooming or a new shoot sprouting. On other days, the progress is less visible, happening beneath the soil. But you know that each day, no matter how small the change, brings you closer to a blossoming garden.

This is the essence of celebrating small wins. It's about acknowledging the progress, whether visible or not, and celebrating the steps you take toward your goal. After all, a journey of a thousand miles begins with a single step. So, let's delve into the power of incremental change and the joy of celebrating small wins.

Recognizing Progress

To understand the importance of this concept, imagine standing in front of a mirror and flexing your muscles a few days after starting your workout regime. At first, the change might not be noticeable. But as you continue your workout, you start to see the results. Your muscles become more defined, your strength increases, and you feel healthier and fitter.

Your transformation from narcissism is similar. At first, the changes might be subtle - a brief pause before reacting, a moment of active listening, a day without seeking validation. But as you continue to practice self-reflection, empathy, and emotional literacy, these small changes accumulate, leading to a noticeable shift in your behavior and attitudes.

Recognizing this progress is crucial. It reinforces your motivation and strengthens your commitment to change. So, take a moment each day to reflect on your progress. What did you do differently today? What changes did you notice in your thoughts, feelings, or behaviors? How did these changes impact your interactions and relationships?

Rewarding Positive Behavior

Now, let's add a dash of fun to this process. Think of a kid who gets a gold star for good behavior, how their eyes light up, how they beam with pride. Rewarding positive behavior works similarly for adults. It provides a sense of achievement and boosts motivation.

So, reward yourself for your progress. Did you manage to handle criticism without getting defensive? Reward yourself with a treat. Did you express empathy in a conversation? Take some time off to enjoy your favorite hobby. Did you set a boundary and stick to it? Indulge in some self-care activities.

These rewards don't have to be grand or expensive. They can be simple pleasures that bring a smile to your face. The key is to associate positive behavior with positive experiences, reinforcing your commitment to change.

Maintaining a Success Journal

Finally, consider keeping a success journal. Just as an artist keeps a portfolio of their best work, a success journal is a collection of your achievements, a record of your progress.

Each day, jot down your successes, however small they might seem. Did you pause and reflect before responding to a provocation? Write it down. Did you actively listen during a conversation without shifting the focus to yourself? Note it down. Did you respect someone else's boundary? Make a record of it.

Over time, this journal will become proof of how far you've come. On challenging days, it will remind you that you've achieved so much and you can keep going, striving, and transforming.

This brings us to the end of this chapter. Remember, the goal is not to become perfect overnight but to make consistent, incremental changes. Each step you take, each change you make, brings you closer to a healthier, more balanced, and empathetic self. So, keep going, keep growing, and keep celebrating your small wins. You're doing great!

Chapter 6

REBUILDING THE BRIDGE: RESTORING RELATIONSHIPS DAMAGED BY NARCISSISM

6

Without a doubt, bridges have been burnt. Think about it.

Can you name 5 people from the top of your head that you wittingly or unwittingly cut off, and the ending wasn't so great? With those people in mind, read through this chapter with the openness to rebuild things or, at the very least, to make amends.

Now, imagine you're an architect, standing before a once majestic bridge, now in disarray. The foundation is shaky; the steel is rusted; cracks and crevices obscure the beauty it once emanated. As an architect, you understand the importance of this bridge, the connection it provides, and the lives it impacts. You know that you can restore this bridge to its former glory with a well-thought-out plan, the right tools, patience, and diligence.

This chapter is your guide to restoring the relationships affected by narcissism. Like the architect, we will address the damage, lay out practical steps for repair, manage expectations, and commit to ongoing maintenance.

6.1 Understanding the Damage: Narcissism in Relationships

Before we dive into the rebuilding process, let's assess the damage. Narcissistic behaviors can leave lasting scars on relationships. Understanding these can help us create a targeted approach to restoration.

Emotional Manipulation

Emotional manipulation has far-reaching consequences, especially creating an atmosphere of confusion and insecurity. The other person may end up feeling like a puppet in your hands, and they may even start distrusting themselves and their emotions.

Lack of Empathy

A lack of empathy can be frustrating and disheartening. It's like talking to a brick wall, your feelings and experiences falling on deaf ears. This lack of empathy can create a chasm in relationships, making the other person feel unseen, unheard, and undervalued.

Violation of Boundaries

If you violate personal boundaries, this means you are disregarding someone's feelings, invading their privacy, or dismissing their needs and wants – generally, this can make the other person lose their sense of identity.

This disrespect for boundaries can lead to a loss of trust and a deep sense of violation.

Gaslighting

As we have seen, gaslighting is a psychological manipulation tactic that you may often employ to distort someone's sense of reality. Although it may seem harmless or like a "game," it can leave the other person doubting their perceptions and even questioning their sanity.

6.2 Practical Steps to Mend Relationships

Rebuilding a damaged relationship is not unlike mending a broken vase. It requires patience, careful handling, and the right adhesive. Here are some practical steps to mend relationships damaged by narcissism:

Apologizing and Showing Remorse

We all stumble, we all make mistakes, and we all falter. It's part of being human. As a narcissist, the road to transformation is laden with missteps. When you've hurt someone with your actions or words, owning up to your mistakes is a significant first step towards mending fences.

A heartfelt apology goes a long way in healing wounds. It's like a soothing balm, alleviating pain and fostering healing. It's an affirmation that you recognize your missteps and are willing to make amends.

However, an apology is more than just saying, 'I'm sorry.' It's about expressing genuine remorse for your actions and their impact on the other person. It's about understanding their hurt and validating their feelings.

Remember, a sincere apology is devoid of excuses or blame-shifting. It's an acknowledgment of your actions, not a justification. It's a commitment to learn from your mistakes and to do better in the future.

Listening and Validating Experiences

Listening is more than just hearing the words spoken; it's about understanding the emotions, experiences, and perspectives behind those words. It's about tuning into their melody amidst the noise of your thoughts, judgments, and biases.

When you listen actively, you create a safe space for the other person to express themselves freely. You convey that their thoughts and feelings matter and that they are seen and heard.

Moreover, validating their experiences shows that you not only listen but also understand and empathize with their feelings. It's an affirmation that their feelings are valid and significant, promoting a sense of acceptance and mutual respect.

Building Trust

Trust is the bedrock of any relationship. It's the glue that binds individuals together, the foundation upon which relationships are built. If your narcissistic behaviors have eroded this trust, rebuilding it requires patience, consistency, and sincerity.

Trust is like a plant; it needs to be nurtured to grow. It requires regular watering with honesty, fertilizing with reliability, and pruning with transparency. You can't rush the process or force it to grow faster. It takes time, effort, and patience to cultivate trust.

Keep your promises, no matter how small. Show up when you say you will. Be honest and transparent in your actions. Over time, these consistent actions will contribute to rebuilding trust.

Remember, trust is not a destination but a continuous journey. It requires consistent effort and diligence to maintain. Keep tending to it, and it will flourish into a lasting bond of trust and mutual respect.

Regular Communication

Express your feelings openly and respectfully. Share your thoughts and experiences, not just about your transformation but also about your daily life. Invite them to share their feelings and experiences, too.

Remember, communication is a two-way street. It involves speaking and listening, expressing and understanding. Maintain this balance to ensure healthy, effective communication.

Ensure your communication is clear, honest, and respectful. Avoid blame, criticism, or defensiveness. Instead, use 'I' statements to express your feelings and thoughts. For instance, instead of saying, "You make me feel ignored," you could say, "I feel ignored when you don't listen to me."

Regular communication keeps you connected, fosters understanding, and resolves misunderstandings. It's the bridge that connects hearts, minds, and souls, making the journey of transformation smoother and more fulfilling.

6.3 Managing Expectations: A Key to Relationship Repair

In the process of mending relationships, it's crucial to manage expectations - both yours and the other person's.

Below are some tips that can help you manage expectations effectively:

Understanding Others' Perspectives

Picture yourself in an art gallery, observing a painting. You're captivated by the colors, the textures, the composition. But what about the artist? How might they have viewed the painting? Was it a burst of joy, a well of sorrow, or a whisper of hope?

Understanding others' perspectives is like viewing a painting through the artist's eyes. It's about seeing beyond our own interpretations and acknowledging that other viewpoints exist. For a narcissist, this can be a pivotal step towards repairing relationships.

Start by putting yourself in the other person's shoes. Try to see the situation from their viewpoint, even if it's different from yours. For example, if a friend felt hurt by your comment, try to understand why they felt that way instead of dismissing their feelings.

Remember, understanding doesn't equate to agreement. You can understand someone's perspective without agreeing with it. The goal is not to change your perspective but to create a space for dialogue, understanding, and respect.

Respecting Boundaries

Think of a soccer field with clear boundary lines. The players move freely within these lines, understanding that stepping out of them disrupts the game. Similarly, every relationship has boundaries - invisible lines that define personal space and comfort.

Respecting boundaries is about acknowledging and honoring these invisible lines. It's about understanding that each person has a right to their personal space, feelings, needs, and autonomy.

For a narcissist, understanding and respecting boundaries can be a challenge. Their self-focused worldview often overlooks others' boundaries. However, you can learn to respect these boundaries with conscious effort and understanding.

Start by asking and understanding the other person's boundaries. It could be about their time, their personal space, or their emotional comfort. Once you understand their boundaries, make a conscious effort to respect them. This shows that you value their comfort and autonomy, fostering trust and mutual respect in the relationship.

Patience and Persistence

Imagine yourself trying to move a mountain. It seems impossible, right? But what if you could move it, one pebble at a time? It might take a while, but eventually, you will see a change. The mountain would start to shift; the landscape would start to transform.

Patience and persistence are about moving this mountain, one pebble at a time. It's about acknowledging that change takes time and that progress might be slow, but every step counts.

For a narcissist, this can be a difficult concept to grasp. You might want quick changes and instant results. But lasting change doesn't work that way. It's a process, often slow and filled with challenges.

So, be patient with yourself and with others. Celebrate your small victories, learn from your setbacks, and keep moving forward. Persistence is the force that keeps you going, even when the road gets tough. It's the grit that helps you move mountains, one pebble at a time.

6.4: Nurturing Relationships: An Ongoing Commitment

Repairing a relationship is just the first step. To maintain a healthy relationship, ongoing care, and nurturing are essential:

Consistent Effort

Nurturing relationships demands conscious, consistent effort. It's not about grand gestures or lofty promises; it's about the little things you do every day.

Perhaps it's a kind word, a listening ear, or a simple act of consideration. Every action counts, and every effort matters. Little by little, these efforts accumulate, strengthening the bond of the relationship.

Open and Honest Communication

Visualize a river that flows freely, unobstructed by dams or blockages. The water is clear, and the current is steady. This is a metaphor for open and honest communication in relationships. It's about letting your thoughts, feelings, and experiences flow freely, unobstructed by fear or pretense.

Speak your truth, express your feelings, and share your experiences. Be clear, be direct, and be genuine. At the same time, lend an ear to the other person. Listen to their words, understand their emotions, and respect their opinions. This two-way flow of communication is the lifeblood of any relationship.

Regular Check-ins

Imagine a lighthouse on a rocky shore, its light providing guidance and assurance to ships in the night. In relationships, regular check-ins serve as this guiding light. They provide a touchpoint, a moment of connection amidst the hustle and bustle of life.

Carve out time for regular check-ins. It could be a daily chat, a weekly dinner, or a monthly outing. Use this time to catch up, to share, to listen, to laugh. These moments of connection weave a strong, resilient fabric of relationship, one that can weather the storms of life.

Mutual Respect and Understanding

Mutual respect and understanding in a relationship is like a dance of acceptance, of valuing each other's individuality while moving together in unity.

Respect the other person's feelings, thoughts, and experiences. Value their uniqueness, their quirks, their dreams. Understand their viewpoints, even if they differ from yours. This mutual respect and understanding create a safe space for both partners to be themselves, fostering a sense of belonging and acceptance.

Building Empathy

Again, building empathy is a lifelong process. Cultivate empathy by stepping into the other person's shoes. Try to understand their feelings, their experiences, their perspective. Respond with kindness and compassion, even when it's hard.

Building empathy is like building a bridge - it requires a strong foundation, the right tools, and a labor of love. But once built, it can transform your relationships, making them deeper, richer, and more fulfilling.

With that, we conclude this chapter on rebuilding relationships affected by narcissism. Remember, relationship repair is not a one-time fix; it's an ongoing process, a continuous journey. It's about consistently putting in the effort, communicating openly, checking in regularly, respecting each other, and cultivating empathy. So, keep tending to your garden of relationships, keep dancing to the rhythm of respect and understanding, and keep building bridges of empathy.

Chapter 7

NAVIGATING THE AFTERMATH OF NARCISSISM

7

Picture yourself standing in a room where everything has been rearranged. The furniture that was once familiar has been shifted to new locations, the walls painted a different color, and even the light seems to filter in differently. Initially, you might feel disoriented, unsure of how to navigate this remodeled space.

But as you spend more time there, you start to adapt. You learn to navigate the new layout, appreciate the fresh paint, and even the light seems comforting in its new angle. This is what life post-change feels like when you begin to shift from narcissism towards empathy.

7.1: Embracing the New Normal: Life Post-Change

As you embrace your new normal, take into consideration the following factors:

Adjusting to Empathetic Interactions

Think back to a time when you learned a new skill, say riding a bicycle. At first, maintaining balance, pedaling, and steering all at once seemed like a Herculean task. But as you practiced, it became second nature. Similarly, empathetic interactions might feel unfamiliar and challenging initially, but with practice, they become an integral part of your social interactions.

Empathy, unlike narcissism, encourages a two-way interaction. It's not just about expressing your feelings but also about understanding and valuing others' emotions. This could mean spending more time listening during conversations, acknowledging others' viewpoints, or considering their feelings before responding.

It might feel awkward at first, like trying to ride a bicycle for the first time, but with practice, it becomes more comfortable and natural.

Navigating Healthy Boundaries

As you transition from narcissism to empathy, understanding and respecting these boundaries become crucial. You learn that every individual, including you, has a personal space that needs to be respected. This could be physical space, emotional space, or even digital space.

For instance, if a friend shares a personal issue, instead of offering unsolicited advice (crossing their emotional boundary), you offer a listening ear (respecting their boundary). Or, if a colleague prefers emails over phone calls for non-urgent matters, you respect their preference (acknowledging their digital boundary).

Navigating these boundaries might seem like walking on a tightrope initially, but over time, it becomes more like driving on a well-marked road, ensuring your relationships are respectful and balanced.

Celebrating Small Victories

Remember the thrill of finding a rare collectible coin or a limited-edition book? It's not about its monetary value but the joy of discovery, the satisfaction of adding it to your collection. Celebrating small victories in your transformation journey offers a similar joy.

Small victories could be anything from successfully managing your defensive reaction to criticism, expressing empathy in a conversation, or respecting a loved one's boundary. Each of these victories signifies progress, a step towards a more empathetic and healthier you.

For instance, during a heated discussion with a friend, you might feel the urge to interrupt and defend your viewpoint (an old narcissistic behavior). But instead, you take a deep breath, listen to their perspective (practicing empathy), and then express your viewpoint respectfully (a small yet significant victory).

So, like a numismatist rejoicing over a newly found rare coin, celebrate these small victories. They are markers of your progress, symbols of your commitment to change, and, most importantly, reminders of your ability to transform and grow.

7.2   Maintaining   Progress: Strategies and Tips

To maintain your progress, the following tips will keep you on track:

Regular Self-reflection

Picture yourself as an explorer mapping an uncharted territory. You traverse new landscapes daily, encounter unexpected challenges, and discover new insights. Self-reflection, in the context of your transformation, is much like mapping this territory. It helps you track your progress, understand your experiences, and gain deeper insights about yourself.

Dedicate some quiet time each day for self-reflection. Reflect on your thoughts, feelings, and actions. Did you handle criticism better today? Were you able to express empathy in your conversations? Were there moments when you slipped into old narcissistic behaviors?

Use a journal to document these reflections. It serves as a record of your progress, a tool for introspection, and a source of motivation. When you write, be honest with yourself. This is not a space for judgment but for understanding and learning.

Mindfulness Practices

Incorporate mindfulness practices into your daily routine. This could be as simple as focusing on your breath, savoring your meals, or immersing yourself in nature. You could also explore formal mindfulness practices like meditation or yoga.

Mindfulness not only reduces stress and improves mental clarity but also enhances empathy. By staying present, you become more attuned to others' feelings and perspectives, fostering deeper connections.

Consistent Therapy Sessions

Therapy can help you maintain your progress as you open up to a professional about your efforts and how much you have achieved. Regular sessions provide a safe space to explore your feelings, confront your fears, and learn new coping strategies.

Your therapist can offer valuable insights, tools, and techniques to maintain your new normal, so be sure to ask them.

Constructive Feedback Acceptance

Feedback, whether from loved ones or a professional, provides an outside perspective on your behaviors and attitudes. It highlights the areas where you're doing well and where you need improvement.

When receiving feedback, keep an open mind and use it as a stepping stone towards change.

Remember, every stroke of the chisel brings the sculptor closer to the masterpiece. Similarly, every piece of constructive feedback brings you closer to your goal - a healthier, more balanced, and empathetic self. So, embrace feedback, learn from it, and let it guide your transformation.

7.3 Dealing with Triggers

Narcissism has its own triggers, whether a person, a word, or a situation. Regardless, it is crucial to identify these triggers so that you can keep them in check:

The Subtle Alarm Bells: Identifying Triggers

Let's imagine walking through a field studded with hidden trapdoors. Each one, when stepped on, triggers an unexpected tumble. However, with a keen eye and careful navigation, you can learn to spot these hidden pitfalls and avoid a potential fall. Similarly, as you navigate the path of transformation, you'll encounter numerous triggers - hidden trapdoors that can lead to a sudden slide back into old narcissistic behaviors.

A trigger could be anything - a casual comment, a specific person, an uncomfortable situation, or even a particular date or time. For instance, receiving criticism could trigger defensiveness, causing a knee-jerk reaction to deny, justify, or shift blame. Alternatively, a demanding situation could trigger an urge to dominate or manipulate, reverting to the familiar power dynamics of narcissism.

The first step in dealing with setbacks is recognizing these triggers. Pay close attention to your emotions, thoughts, and reactions in different situations. Notice when you feel the tug of old patterns, the stirrings of narcissistic tendencies. This awareness is your compass, helping you navigate the field of transformation and avoid potential pitfalls.

What are your triggers?

____

____

____

____

____

____

____

____

____

Armoring Up: Cultivating Coping Strategies

Once you've identified potential triggers, the next step is to develop strategies to cope with them healthily and productively. Each person's coping mechanism could be different, much like a customized suit of armor. It's about figuring out what works best for you.

For instance, if receiving criticism is a trigger, a coping strategy could be to pause and take a few deep breaths before responding, allowing you to react in a more thoughtful and less defensive manner. If a particular person or situation triggers your narcissistic tendencies, you could practice mindfulness techniques to stay present and avoid falling into old patterns.

Remember, the goal is not to avoid triggers but to manage them effectively. It's about wearing your armor of coping strategies, so you're better equipped to handle the battles of transformation.

The Power of Allies: Leaning on Support

Support can come in various forms - a patient listener, a comforting shoulder, a wise guide, or even a cheerleader. It could be a family member, a close friend, a support group, or a mental health professional. The key is to reach out and lean on this support, especially during challenging times.

When faced with setbacks, instead of isolating yourself or dwelling on the negative, reach out to your support system. Share your feelings, ask for advice, or simply spend time with them. Knowing that you're not alone and have people who care about you and believe in you can make the journey less daunting and more manageable.

Of course, seeking support doesn't mean relying solely on others. It's equally important to be there for yourself, to believe in your strength, and to be your own cheerleader. After all, you are the hero of your transformation story, and every hero needs a supportive sidekick, even if it's their own self.

As we traverse through this chapter, remember that setbacks are not roadblocks but stepping stones on your path to transformation. They are opportunities to learn, to grow, and to strengthen your resolve.

7.4 Lifelong Learning: Your Commitment to Growth

Eliminating narcissism is not a one-off thing. You have to be consistently committed to self-improvement, no matter how progressed you feel:

Continuous Self-improvement

Think about a tree, an ever-growing entity that sprawls its branches towards the sky, deepens its roots into the earth, and unfurls new leaves with each passing season. This is the essence of continuous self-improvement, an unending process of growth and development.

As you transition from narcissism to empathy, the commitment to self-improvement becomes a cornerstone. It's about striving to be better today than you were yesterday, to learn from each experience, and to constantly evolve.

Perhaps it's about cultivating patience in difficult situations, developing better listening skills, or managing your reactions more effectively. Each day offers a fresh opportunity for learning and growth, a new leaf on your tree of transformation.

Active Participation in Therapy

Active participation in therapy sessions is crucial to reap the maximum benefits. It involves more than just attending sessions. It's about applying the insights and strategies discussed in the sessions to your daily life.

It might mean practicing a mindfulness technique you learned during a session or reflecting on a meaningful discussion. It's about making therapy a part of your life, not just an hour in your weekly schedule.

Regular Reading and Research

Regular reading and research keep you informed about the latest insights on narcissism, empathy, and mental health. It helps you understand different perspectives, learn new strategies, and stay motivated on your path.

It could be a self-help book, an insightful article, a research paper, or even a thought-provoking podcast. The idea is to feed your mind with knowledge, fuel your transformation with insights, and fortify your commitment to growth.

Attending Relevant Workshops and Seminars

Workshops and seminars offer a platform to learn from experts, share experiences, and connect with others on a similar path. You get to explore new concepts, engage in stimulating discussions, and even challenge your own beliefs.

Whether it's a workshop on emotional intelligence, a seminar on mindfulness, or a group therapy session, each experience adds a brick to your edifice of transformation.

Up next, we dive deeper into how you can visualize a narcissism-free future!

Chapter 8

TURNING THE PAGE: ENVISIONING A NARCISSISM-FREE FUTURE

8

Have you ever heard about the power of visualization? This means holding a crystal-clear picture of your desires in your mind and working toward it. Envisioning a narcissism-free future opens you up to opportunities, possibilities, and hope, and this chapter will show you how to do this:

Setting Personal Goals

Your goals could range from improving your listening skills, developing empathy, and fostering healthier relationships to practicing self-reflection regularly. Remember to make your goals SMART - Specific, Measurable, Attainable, Relevant, and Time-bound. This ensures that your goals are clear, achievable, and aligned with your overall vision.

For instance, instead of setting a vague goal like "I want to improve my listening skills," you could set a SMART goal like "I will practice active listening for 15 minutes each day during conversations for the next month." This goal is specific (active listening), measurable (15 minutes), attainable (with daily practice), relevant (improves communication), and time-bound (next month).

Visualizing Improved Relationships

Think about watching a movie in your mind, a movie of your life. But in this movie, your relationships are healthier, more balanced, and more fulfilling. Visualizing these improved relationships can fuel your motivation and guide your actions.

Imagine having a conversation where you actively listen, understand, and validate the other person's feelings. Picture yourself dealing with criticism calmly and constructively. Visualize setting healthy boundaries and respecting those of others.

This visualization is not a fantasy but a preview of the possibilities. It's a beacon that guides your actions and decisions towards healthier relationships.

Imagining a More Empathetic Self

Now, let's turn the spotlight on you. Imagine looking in the mirror and seeing a more empathetic version of yourself. This reflection is not a stranger but the person you are becoming.

In this mirror, you see yourself actively tuning into others' feelings, validating their experiences, and responding with understanding. You see yourself respecting personal boundaries, managing your reactions healthily, and embracing open, honest communication. You see a version of you that's not just self-aware but also understanding and considerate of others.

This reflection is not an illusion but a glimpse of your potential. It's an affirmation of your capability to change, grow, and become more empathetic.

As you envision this narcissism-free future, remember that it's not a distant dream but a tangible reality within your reach. With each goal you set, each visualization you create, and each reflection you observe, you're stepping closer to this reality.

You're not just turning the page on narcissism; you're writing a new chapter, a chapter full of growth, transformation, and empathy. So, pick up your pen, gaze at your horizon, and start writing. Your future is waiting.

8.1 Healing: A Passage to Renewal

Healing starts with acknowledgment and forgiveness. Let's see how you can achieve both in this section:

Acknowledging Past Mistakes

Imagine standing before a canvas filled with strokes of your past actions, a palette of experiences that have shaped your journey so far. Among these colors, some might stand out, representing the mistakes you've made. Recognizing these elements is not about dwelling in regret but about owning your past, and acknowledging your missteps.

Think about the instances where your narcissistic behaviors might have caused pain to others. The times when your need for admiration overshadowed someone else's feelings, when your lack of empathy created a chasm in your relationships, or when your fear of criticism led to defensive reactions.

Reflecting on these instances is not an exercise in self-blame or guilt but a step toward understanding and acceptance. It's about acknowledging that these were mistakes, not because they define you, but because they were stepping stones in your path towards growth.

Forgiving Self and Others

Now, think of a tightly clenched fist, holding on to a stone. The grip is firm, the knuckles white, the effort exhausting. Holding onto past mistakes and hurts is much like holding on to this stone - it's tiring, and it keeps you stuck in the past. Forgiveness is about opening this clenched fist, letting go of the stone, and freeing yourself from the burden of the past.

Begin by forgiving yourself. Understand that everyone makes mistakes, and that's how we learn and grow. You're not the same person who made those mistakes; you've grown, you've learned, and you're on a path to becoming a better version of yourself.

Next, consider forgiving others who might have contributed to your narcissistic behaviors. They, too, are flawed human beings who make mistakes. Holding onto resentment only hurts you and hinders your progress. Letting go doesn't mean forgetting or condoning their actions; it means freeing yourself from the chains of resentment and anger.

Remember, forgiveness is not a one-time act but a continuous process. It's a choice you make every day, a choice to let go, to free yourself, and to move forward.

Embracing the Healing Process

Picture a river, flowing gently, carving its path with persistence and grace. Over time, it transforms the landscape, creating valleys, moving mountains, and nourishing life. Your healing process is like this river, a continual flow that gradually transforms you, nourishing your growth and well-being.

Embrace this process with patience and kindness. There might be times of rapid flow when you see noticeable progress. Other times, the flow might be slow, almost imperceptible, but remember, even then, you're moving forward.

Healing is not about erasing your past or changing your core self. It's about transforming unhealthy patterns, fostering healthier relationships, and becoming more empathetic and balanced.

As you navigate this passage of healing, remember to be kind to yourself. Celebrate your progress, learn from your setbacks, and have faith in your ability to heal and grow. After all, you're not just a passive spectator in this process; you're the river, carving your path, shaping your journey, and nourishing your own transformation.

8.2 The Role of External Support

As much as this is a personal journey, you still don't have to do it alone. You can seek the support of other individuals, for instance, a mental health professional (which we've already covered) or people who are on the same path as you:

Joining Support Groups

Support groups can be thought of as a campfire in the wilderness of transformation. Gathered around this campfire are others like you, each on their path of change, each with their story. The fire crackles, the stories unfold, and in the shared warmth and light, you find solace, support, and strength.

In a support group, you're not alone. You're part of a community of learners, a team of adventurers, each navigating their transformation. You share your experiences, your challenges, and your victories. You listen to others, learn from their journeys, and draw inspiration from their courage.

Each meeting, each conversation, is an opportunity to learn, to connect, to grow. In this give and take, you find a sense of belonging, a sense of companionship, and a sense of purpose.

Engaging in Personal Development Programs

Personal development programs, much like a compass, provide direction, guide your steps, and help you stay on course.

They are designed to enhance various aspects of your life - be it emotional intelligence, interpersonal skills, stress management, or self-awareness. They offer practical tools, actionable strategies, and valuable insights to foster personal growth and improvement.

As you engage in these programs, you equip yourself with the skills and knowledge to navigate your transformation. You learn to manage your emotions, to communicate effectively, to build empathy. Each program, each lesson, is a milestone on your path, a guidepost pointing towards your destination.

Don't be afraid to reach out, connect, and engage with others.

8.3 Building a Supportive Network: Friends, Family, and Allies

Start this process by reaching out to those you've hurt or pushed away. Recall what we said about building bridges and opening the lines of communication. It could be a simple text, a letter, or a face-to-face conversation. Express your remorse for past actions and your commitment to change.

Initiate actions that demonstrate your transformation. Show empathy in your conversations, respect their boundaries, and respond to their needs. Prove through consistent actions that you're making a genuine effort to change.

Keep in mind that the process of rebuilding relationships won't happen overnight. It's like renovating a house - it takes time, patience, and consistent effort. But the result - a warm, harmonious relationship - is worth every bit of effort.

Forming New, Healthy Connections

Now, visualize yourself at a social gathering, surrounded by people, most of them strangers. You strike up a conversation with someone, finding common interests and shared experiences. Over time, these casual interactions can blossom into genuine friendships. As you step away from narcissism, forming new, healthy connections plays a vital part.

Start by putting your newfound empathy skills to use. Show genuine interest in others, listen actively, and respond with understanding. Be open to their perspectives, even if they differ from yours.

Find common interests that can serve as a foundation for new friendships. It could be a shared love for books, a common hobby, or a shared passion for a cause.

Remember, forming new connections is not about seeking admiration or validation but about building mutually enriching relationships. It's about giving and receiving, understanding and being understood, caring and being cared for.

Cultivating a Supportive Environment

Surround yourself with people who support your growth, understand your transformation, and positively enrich your life. It could be family members encouraging your efforts, friends cheering your progress, or mentors guiding your path.

Create an atmosphere of open communication where feelings are shared, experiences are discussed, and feedback is welcomed.

Engage in activities that foster growth and well-being. It could be a group therapy session, a mindfulness workshop, or simply a quiet evening spent journaling.

Remember, the environment you cultivate plays a significant role in your transformation. A supportive, nurturing environment accelerates your growth and makes the process more fulfilling.

In the grand scheme of things, building a supportive network is akin to constructing a safety net. As you trapeze through the exhilarating yet challenging circus of transformation, this network provides you with a safety net, catching you when you stumble and propelling you to greater heights. So, reach out, connect, and build your network.

After all, no one is an island, and transformation is easier (and much more fun) when you're in good company. Now that we've laid the groundwork in this chapter let's look a little into the stigma and myths surrounding narcissism.

Chapter 9

DISARMING THE NARCISSIST'S STIGMA: MYTHS, REALITIES, AND THE POWER OF UNDERSTANDING

9

Imagine you're at a dinner party, and the conversation turns to personality types. Someone brings up the term 'narcissist,' and immediately, the atmosphere shifts. There's a murmur of agreement as people share anecdotes and stereotypes about narcissistic individuals - they're selfish, they don't care about others, they're beyond help.

As you listen, a knot forms in your stomach. You recognize these misconceptions because you've been on the receiving end of them. It's time to set the record straight, challenge these myths, and shed light on the realities of narcissism.

9.1 The Stigma of Narcissism: Myths and Realities

Let's start with the most common myth: Narcissists are selfish, with no regard for others. While it's true that narcissists can exhibit self-centered behaviors, it's critical to remember that this stems from deep-rooted insecurities and fears. It's not a choice you make but a coping mechanism you've developed.

Another myth is that narcissists lack emotions. On the contrary, many narcissists experience intense emotions but struggle to express them appropriately. Picture a tumultuous sea hidden beneath a calm surface - that's the emotional landscape of a narcissist.

Then there's the belief that narcissists are incapable of change, written off as lost causes. But this is as baseless as claiming that a chameleon can't change its colors. With the right support, understanding, and commitment to change, narcissists can indeed break away from their old patterns of behavior and learn healthier ways of interacting with the world.

Sharing Personal Experiences

Sharing personal experiences can be a powerful way to challenge these misconceptions. It's like bringing a backstage tour of a theater performance - offering a glimpse into the behind-the-scenes realities that often remain unseen.

For example, you can share how you've grappled with feelings of insecurity and fear, which may have manifested as narcissistic behaviors. Talk about the intense emotions you've experienced and the challenges you've faced in expressing them.

Describe your efforts to change - the therapy sessions, the self-reflection, the consistent efforts to build empathy and respect boundaries. Your experiences can provide a first-hand account of the complexities, challenges, and possibilities of overcoming narcissism.

Educating Others about Narcissism

Think of yourself as a tour guide, educating curious travelers about a new city. Your role is to provide accurate information, clarify misconceptions, and enhance their understanding. In the context of narcissism, you can become an educator, guiding others towards a more accurate and empathetic understanding of narcissism.

Start by explaining what narcissism is - a personality pattern characterized by certain behaviors and not a conscious choice. Discuss the different types of narcissism, highlighting that it exists on a spectrum.

Explain the underlying insecurities and fears that often fuel narcissistic behaviors. It's like pulling back the curtain on a magic show, revealing the mechanisms behind the illusion.

Also, share about the potential for change. Talk about the role of therapy, the power of self-awareness, and the process of learning new behaviors.

By educating others about narcissism, you can help dispel myths, foster understanding, and challenge the stigma associated with it.

9.2 Advocacy and Awareness: The Narcissist's Role

Participating in Awareness Campaigns

Imagine a marathon, a sea of people, each running for a cause close to their heart. Each step they take, each mile they conquer, raises awareness for their chosen cause, rallying support and sparking conversations. As an individual who has walked the path from narcissism to empathy, you, too, can join this marathon of change, participating in awareness campaigns that bring attention to the complexities of narcissism.

There are numerous ways to participate in awareness campaigns. You could join a walk, run, or cycle event dedicated to mental health awareness. You could take part in social media campaigns, sharing posts and videos that shed light on narcissism. Or, you could organize an event in your local community, inviting speakers, hosting discussions, and creating a platform for dialogue and understanding.

Participating in such campaigns not only raises awareness but also challenges the stigma associated with narcissism. It sends a powerful message - that narcissism is not a label to be feared or shunned but a condition to be understood, addressed, and transformed.

Sharing Knowledge and Insights

Sharing your knowledge and insights about narcissism can take many forms. You could write a blog, sharing your personal experiences and learnings. You could give a talk at a local school or community center, educating others about the realities of narcissism. Or, you could participate in a panel discussion or a podcast, offering your unique perspective.

When you share your knowledge, you not only educate others but also empower them. You empower those who might be struggling with narcissistic tendencies to seek help and embrace change. You empower their loved ones to understand, support, and empathize. You empower society to replace judgment with understanding and stigma with acceptance.

Advocating for Mental Health Support

Advocating for mental health support involves raising your voice for better mental health policies in workplaces and educational institutions. It's about championing the importance of therapy and counseling, and making these services more accessible and affordable. It's about fighting the stigma associated with seeking mental health support promoting a culture of acceptance and understanding.

Your advocacy can make a tangible difference in the lives of those dealing with narcissism. It can lead to more supportive environments, better access to mental health services, and a shift in societal attitudes towards mental health. In this advocacy, you're not just speaking up for yourself but for countless others who might be walking the same path, seeking the same change, yearning for the same understanding.

9.3 Changing Society's View: A Collective Effort

Collaborating with Mental Health Organizations

Picture yourself as part of a dynamic and motivated team, all working towards a common goal. The energy is infectious, the synergy palpable, and the collective impact significant. As an individual who has walked the path from narcissism to empathy, you can be part of such a team, collaborating with mental health organizations to change society's view of narcissism.

Being a part of such collaborations can have a profound impact. You could contribute your insights to awareness campaigns, lend your voice to advocacy initiatives, or even help design resources for individuals dealing with narcissism.

These collaborations serve a dual purpose. They not only amplify the reach and impact of your efforts but also provide you with a platform to learn, grow, and contribute on a larger scale.

Working with mental health organizations, you can help bring about policy changes, influence societal attitudes, and make mental health a mainstream conversation. And in doing so, you're not just changing society's view of narcissism; you're also contributing to a more inclusive, empathetic, and understanding world.

Encouraging Open Conversations about Narcissism

Visualize a world where conversations about mental health are as common and accepted as discussions about the weather – no stigma, no judgment, just open, honest dialogue. As an individual who has firsthand experience with narcissism, you can play a key role in creating this world, encouraging open conversations about narcissism.

Start with your own circles. Bring up the topic in your conversations with friends, family, and colleagues. Share your experiences, insights, and learnings. Let them know that it's okay to talk about mental health, to ask questions, and to seek help.

Create safe spaces for these conversations. It could be a book club discussing a novel featuring a character with narcissism, a coffee meet-up dedicated to mental health discussions, or even a digital forum where people can share their thoughts and experiences.

By encouraging open conversations about narcissism, you're not just challenging the stigma; you're also creating a ripple effect. Each conversation leads to another, each shared insight opens a mind, and each question asked paves the way for understanding.

Promoting Empathy and Understanding

Imagine a world where empathy is as ubiquitous as air, where understanding is the norm, not the exception.

This might seem like a tall order, but as an individual who has navigated the transformation from narcissism to empathy, you can play a pivotal role in promoting empathy and understanding.

Lead by example. Show empathy in your interactions, strive to understand others' perspectives, and respond with kindness and respect. Your actions can inspire others, showing them what empathy looks like in action.

Educate others about the importance of empathy, not just for individuals dealing with narcissism, but for everyone. Talk about the benefits of empathy - how it strengthens relationships, fosters emotional well-being, and builds stronger, more compassionate communities.

Remember, promoting empathy is about creating a world where everyone feels seen, heard, and valued.

9.4 Leaving a Legacy: The Narcissist's Contribution

Picture an auditorium filled with people, their eyes fixed on you, their ears tuned to your words. You're sharing your story, your transformation from narcissism to empathy. Each word, each sentence, and each pause resonates with the audience, striking a chord and sparking a thought. This is the power of your personal story, a beacon of hope and inspiration for others navigating a similar path.

Your story is not just about the struggles, the challenges, or the setbacks. It's about the triumphs, the victories, the progress. It's about the moments of clarity, the insights gained, and the lessons learned. It's about the courage to change, the commitment to growth, and resilience in the face of adversity.

By sharing your story, you're not just expressing yourself; you're inspiring others. You're showing them that change is possible, growth is achievable, and a better future awaits. Your story is a testament to the power of self-awareness, the value of empathy, and the potential of transformation.

Contributing to Mental Health Research

Your contribution to mental health research can make a significant difference. It can provide a first-hand perspective, a lived experience that complements empirical data. It can offer insights into the realities of narcissism, the nuances of empathy, and the dynamics of change.

By contributing to mental health research, you're not just enhancing scientific knowledge; you're also affecting lives. You're helping shape interventions, influence therapies, and improve mental health services. Your contribution is a ripple in the ocean of mental health research, creating waves that can reach far and wide.

Mentoring Others on the Same Path

Finally, envision yourself as a mentor, guiding a protégé on their path of transformation. You're there to support them, encourage them, and guide them. Your experiences serve as lessons, your insights as guidance, and your transformation as inspiration.

As a mentor, you have the unique opportunity to make a tangible difference in someone's life. You can provide practical advice, emotional support, and motivational nudges. You can share your strategies, discuss your challenges, and celebrate your victories together.

By mentoring others on the same path, you're not just helping them transform; you're also reinforcing your own growth. You're reflecting on your journey, reaffirming your commitment to change, and consolidating your learnings. Your role as a mentor is not just a contribution to others but also a gift to yourself.

Now, as we pause here, reflect on the legacy you're building. Your story inspires others, your contribution enriches research, and your mentorship guides transformation. Each step you take, each word you share, and each insight you offer is leaving a mark and, hopefully, making a difference.

CONCLUSION

Conclusion

As we reach the end of our shared journey, it's time to reflect on the miles we've traveled together. We've navigated the stormy seas of narcissism, delved into its depths, and surfaced with a deeper understanding and empathy. Together, we've discovered that narcissism is not a life sentence but a starting point for transformation.

Key Takeaways: Lessons and Insights

Throughout our journey, we've collected a treasure trove of lessons and insights. We've learned that narcissism, though complex, can be understood and addressed. We've learned the power of empathy, the value of self-awareness, and the strength of vulnerability. We've discovered the importance of setting healthy boundaries, the significance of active listening, and the impact of sincere apologies.

A Final Note: Call to Action

Now, as we stand on the brink of our parting, I'd like to leave you with a call to action. Not a command but an invitation. An invitation to continue exploring, learning, and growing. To take the insights from our journey and apply them to your own life.

Remember, transformation is not a destination but a journey. It's not about sudden leaps but consistent steps. So, don't rush, don't push, just keep moving forward, one step at a time. And always remember, you're not alone in this journey. Reach out when you need support, lean on your allies, and remember to be kind to yourself.

Resources for Further Exploration

The end of our journey should not be an end to your exploration. There are countless resources out there to support you - books, articles, podcasts, therapy sessions, and support groups. Seek them out, learn from them, and let them guide your ongoing journey. And remember, every resource you explore, every insight you gain, is another step towards your transformation.

As we bid goodbye, I want you to know that I'm incredibly proud of you. Proud of your courage to embark on this journey, your resilience in the face of challenges, and your commitment to change. Keep going, keep growing, and remember, you're not just transforming yourself; you're transforming the world around you, one empathetic interaction at a time.

Share Your Thoughts

Dear Readers,

I am writing to express my deepest gratitude for your support in reading my book. Your time and engagement mean the world to me. If you've enjoyed the journey through these pages, please consider leaving a review. Your words can guide and inspire other readers, helping them discover the book and decide if it's the right fit for them.

Reviews are the lifeblood of independent authors, and your honest feedback can make a significant impact. Thank you for being a part of my literary journey, and I look forward to hearing from you.

To submit a review, kindly navigate to your Order History, locate the book in your purchased items, and select 'Write a Product Review.'

With gratitude,

Joyce T.

Bonus Gift

As a modest gesture to express my gratitude, I'm offering you a complimentary of my bundle e-book that will play a vital role in enhancing your success with this book:

Healing Haven 2-in-1 Bundle

Highly Sensitive Empath vs. Narcissistic Individual Unveiled + The Narcissist's Journey to Healing :

A Comprehensive Guide to Recognize, Navigate, and Flourish in Relationships with these Contrasting Personalities

Scan QR code to download with Access Code: healing

www.JoyceTbooks.com

REFERENCES

- Narcissism | Definition, Origins, Pathology, Behavior, Traits ...
  https://www.britannica.com/science/narcissism

- How to Recognize a Covert Narcissist
  https://www.verywellmind.com/understanding-the-covert-narcissist-4584587

- 6 Keys for Narcissists to Change Toward the Higher Self
  https://www.psychologytoday.com/us/blog/communication-success/201410/6-keys-narcissists-change-toward-the-higher-self

- Can Narcissists Learn Empathy
  https://www.businessinsider.com/can-narcissists-learn-empathy-2018-8

- Narcissistic personality disorder: effect on relationships

  https://pubmed.ncbi.nlm.nih.gov/23472440/

- Impact of narcissistic leadership on employee work outcomes ...

  https://fbj.springeropen.com/articles/10.118
  6/s43093-020-00040-x

- Narcissistic Personality Disorder: Symptoms & Treatment

  https://my.clevelandclinic.org/health/disease
  s/9742-narcissistic-personality-disorder

- 6 Keys for Narcissists to Change Toward the Higher Self

  https://www.psychologytoday.com/us/blog/c
  ommunication-success/201410/6-keys-
  narcissists-change-toward-the-higher-self

- Gaslighting Examples: 17 Things Abusers Will Say

https://www.insider.com/guides/health/sex-relationships/gaslighting-examples

- How to Confront Narcissists' Lethal Weapon: Projection

  https://www.psychologytoday.com/us/blog/toxic-relationships/201903/how-confront-narcissists-lethal-weapon-projection

- The Role Of Triangulation In The Narcissistic Abuse Cycle

  https://www.narcissisticabuserehab.com/triangulation-narcissistic-abuse-cycle/

- Narcissistic Abuse Cycle: Stages, Impact, and Coping

  https://www.verywellmind.com/narcissistic-abuse-cycle-stages-impact-and-coping-6363187

- 6 Signs That You Might Be a Vulnerable Narcissist

  https://www.psychologytoday.com/us/blog/t

he-superhuman-mind/202003/6-signs-that-
you-might-be-a-vulnerable-narcissist

- Understanding and mitigating narcissists' low
  empathy
  https://www.researchgate.net/publication/31
  9271914_Understanding_and_mitigating_na
  rcissists'_low_empathy

- Self aware narcissists here's how to work on
  your empathy skills
  https://www.youtube.com/watch?v=PuV3hu
  89FhE

- 17 Empathy Prompts for Narcissists
  https://innertoxicrelief.com/empathy-
  challenges-for-narcissists/

- Self-awareness and introspection in
  Narcissistic ...
  https://www.peertechzpublications.org/articl
  es/APT-5-126.php

- A Guide To Cognitive Behavioral Therapy For Narcissistic ...
  https://www.betterhelp.com/advice/therapy/a-guide-to-cognitive-behavioral-therapy-for-narcissistic-personality-disorder/

- Narcissistic Personality Disorder: The Treatment Challenge
  https://psychnews.psychiatryonline.org/doi/full/10.1176/appi.pn.2016.5a19

- The Power of Small Wins
  https://hbr.org/2011/05/the-power-of-small-wins

- Narcissistic Traits and Their Impact on Relationships
  https://www.psychologytoday.com/us/blog/coping-during-crisis/202205/narcissistic-traits-and-their-impact-relationships

- How to Apologize Sincerely and Effectively
  https://www.verywellmind.com/how-to-apologize-more-sincerely-3144467

- 12 Concrete Steps To Communicate Better In Relationships
  https://www.mindbodygreen.com/articles/how-to-communicate-better-in-relationships

- How to Develop Empathy in Your Relationships
  https://www.verywellmind.com/how-to-develop-empathy-in-relationships-1717547

- Confessions of a Recovering Narcissist-Or How I Learned ...
  https://goodmenproject.com/featured-content/confessions-of-a-recovering-narcissist-or-how-i-learned-to-be-unselfish/

- The Secret to a Happy Relationship Is Empathy
  https://www.psychologytoday.com/us/blog/

mindful-anger/202003/the-secret-happy-relationship-is-empathy

- 9 Tips, Tools, and Strategies for Narcissistic Abuse Recovery https://www.healthline.com/health/mental-health/9-tips-for-narcissistic-abuse-recovery

- Resilience in Mental Health Recovery: Dealing with Setbacks https://www.healthyplace.com/blogs/recoveringfrommentalillness/2022/11/resilience-in-mental-health-recovery-dealing-with-setbacks

- How to Stop Being a Narcissist: 21 Tips https://www.choosingtherapy.com/how-to-stop-being-a-narcissist/

- Narcissistic personality disorder - Diagnosis and treatment https://www.mayoclinic.org/diseases-conditions/narcissistic-personality-disorder/diagnosis-treatment/drc-20366690

- The Importance of Having a Support System
  https://www.mentalhealthfirstaid.org/2020/08/the-importance-of-having-a-support-system/

- Forgiving Yourself After Narcissistic Abuse
  https://www.psychopathfree.com/articles/forgiving-yourself-after-narcissistic-abuse.366/

- 7 Myths About Narcissistic Personality Disorder
  https://www.psychologytoday.com/us/blog/understanding-narcissism/202102/7-myths-about-narcissistic-personality-disorder

- World Narcissistic Abuse Awareness Day 2017 to Feature ...
  https://www.prnewswire.com/news-releases/world-narcissistic-abuse-awareness-day-2017-to-feature-free-week-long-telesummit-300459442.html

- The Stigma Behind Narcissistic Personality
  Disorder

  https://www.sokyahealth.com/connection/re
  ducing-the-stigma-behind-narcissistic-
  personality-disorder/

- Narcissistic Personality Disorder in Clinical ...
  https://www.ncbi.nlm.nih.gov/pmc/articles/
  PMC5819598/